The Hce

The Home Place

Meditations On An
Ozark Life

by
Fayrene Stafford Farmer

First Printing 1997
Second Printing 1998

Printed in the USA
By Litho Printers & Bindery
Cassville, Missouri

DEDICATION

To my husband, Gaylord, who has loved me unconditionally for nearly half a century.

To my children, Gerald, Danny and Alice Gaye, who became wise, productive adults despite a mother who loved them deeply, but not always wisely.

To my grandsons, John-Mark Farmer Zini and Dylan Hunter Zini, who have given our family an abundance of joy, laughter, and love lessons.

ACKNOWLEDGMENTS

MY SINCEREST THANKS to Lin Wellford, best selling author, talented artist and friend, for the cover design and all other art work. Her help is proof that even the weak can walk on water if a confident hand is extended.

My deep appreciation to Adelia Croley, Marguerite Iller, and Yvonne Herron for reading the manuscript and for their thoughtful comments and ideas.

A special thanks to the readers of Nubbin Ridge for rooting, prodding and cheering me on until I finally wrote the book.

Prayers and blessings to Sue, Susan, Arbie, Char, Jackie and Yvonne, The Thursday Prayer Group, for encouragement and spiritual guidance.

I am much obliged to Betty Anderson, full-time farm woman and part-time typesetter, whose loyalty and expertise have been invaluable as this was my "first time out of the chute."

Illustrations: Lin Wellford

Proof Readers: Adelia Croley
                      Marguerite Iller
                      Yvonne Herron

Typesetting & Layout:
                      Betty Anderson
                      D & B Farms Typesetting & Design
                      4934 CR 422· Berryville, AR 72616

PREFACE

The family farm has joined the list of endangered species. The life we live on our hill is in danger of becoming extinct. It is a simple life, a life of natural beauty, solitude, and an awareness of the daily presence of God.

A trip to the woods or a walk along the banks of Yocum Creek isn't to escape problems but to rest my mind to deal with them later.

We have lived here for a long time. Our two sons and a daughter have grown up here and left. And always I have found the words of Job to be true. "Speak to the earth and it will teach you."

I walk down the Valley of Silence,
Down the dim voiceless valley alone,
And I hear not the sound of a footstep
Around me, but God's and my own;
And the hush of my heart is as holy
As bowers whence angels have flown.

(The song of a mystic)

CONTENTS

SECTION IV *"Grandkids"*

SECTION V *"Mama's Scrapbook"*

You will go out in joy
and be lead forth in peace;
The mountain and hills
will burst forth into song before you,
And all the trees of the field
will clap their hands.

Isaiah 55:12

Lookin' Back

Distilled Memories

For we are God's workmanship, created in Christ Jesus to do good works, prepared in advance for us to do. Ephesians 2:10

Memory is evoked in many ways. Who of us cannot recall the smell of the classroom where we spent our early years or the softness of the skin of a newborn baby?

I would wish, when I am old to hold forever the sounds and smells of Nubbin Ridge.

They would be reminders of a sometimes lonely, often times delightful and always rewarding life.

The sounds I would preserve would not only be the soft mooing of a mama cow or the poignant cry of a flock of wild geese but also the voice of a corral gate complaining in a rusty tenor upon being opened or closed.

The familiar sound of my husband's old pickup truck chugging into the driveway just at dark as well as metal scraping across flint rocks as the stock trailer is pulled across the cow pasture I would also like to remember forever.

If I had the ability to capture in a bottle the sweet aroma of a barn filled with freshly cut June hay and could share it with others it could possibly be ranked as the eighth wonder of the world.

Livestock auction odors which linger on my husband's clothes long after the auction is over and which are a mixture of cow manure and stale cigarette smoke could someday become a pleasant memory.

Yes, if I could just come up with a way to save these parts of my life I could carry them in tiny flasks buried deeply in my purse. And then when I finally sat, bowed low with age, an object of pity in some far-off nursing home I would uncap my little bottles one by one. Whispering softly to my young, impatient caretakers I would say, "Life was not always thus, my dears, life was not always thus."

The Hackadackles

If any of you lack wisdom, let him ask of God, that giveth to all men liberally, and upbraideth not; and it shall be given him. James 1:5

They are women. They can be seen alone or in groups. In church they often sit in the front pews. Over thirty years ago, probably before the term "Senior Citizen" was born, my great nephew, Wesley, who delighted in coining new words, gave these women a name. In Wesley's four-year-old mind they became the Hackadackles.

I was a young woman myself at that time and thought Wesley's word was cute and the women themselves rather amusing. How could anyone get so stooped, so short and so thin of hair that a tiny patch of pink scalp peeped through the carefully coiffured hairdo?

Now at age sixty-four, with a touch of osteoporosis, I have shrunk an inch or two, what is left of my once brown hair is white and I am finding that it is virtually impossible to hold my shoulders back for any length of time. I am a Hackadackle.

Many of the women of my generation, including famous women, are finding themselves Hackadackles as well. Elizabeth Taylor, whose acting in National Velvet made every little girl long for a pony, had hip replacement surgery recently, Dinah Shore, who could sing "Carolina in the Morning" like I have never heard it sung before or since, is dead, and Jacqueline Kennedy Onassis, our role model in the days of Camelot, even down to our copying her little pillbox hat, had a form of cancer common to women over age fifty.

But you know what? I am proud to be a Hackadackle. I just hope that I am worthy to be called one. Many are the most courageous people I know. Some have lost husbands and children and frequently their own health but they never, ever give up. Most of these women get up every morning in spite of physical pain and loneliness and face the world with a smile.

They have learned that the ending of life is quite different from the beginning but they get pleasure from it anyway and in so doing bring joy to others as well.

What has been the best time of your life?" I asked my ninety-two year old friend, Thelma. With eyes twinkling and a sweet smile she replied, "Why, today of course." A fine Hackadackle, my friend, Thelma.

The Barn That Would Not Die

Honor your Father and your Mother, which is the first
commandment with a promise. Ephesians 6:2

Once upon a time, many years ago, north of the town of Green Forest, at the intersection of a country road known as Cisco and Arkansas Highway 103, there stood a sprawling white farmhouse. Inside that house lived a family: a father, a mother and five children.

Behind the old house, protecting the family from the harsh west winds of winter, stood a barn. The father of the family took great pride in the big barn, painting it red with white trim, placing a galloping weather vane atop the steep tin roof and even writing his own initials, "C J S" in large black letters inside the entrance way.

Over the years, as it always happens, the children grew up and moved away to homes of their own. The parents remained, but the strength of their youth declined with each passing year.

One day, the old white farmhouse burned. The couple, who were very old by now, lived out the rest of their years in a smart new bungalow.

The red barn remained to mark the spot where a vibrant happy family had once lived, worked, laughed and played and where the children never dreamed that it would not always be so.

Even though the property was eventually sold, the sight of the red barn in the ensuing years brought back a flood of memories to the children who once lived there, especially to the youngest child, a girl.

She recalled her father, with perspiration stains on his khaki work shirt, standing tall and straight in the wagon bed as he drove the work horses into the barn after a hard day in the fields.

She remembered herself as a preschooler, barefoot and clad in a feed sack dress, wiggling under the barn floor in search of a litter of kittens.

She recalled in later years, climbing steps to the barn loft on rainy days with a book in hand to read the hours away while the rain comforted her with its steady beat on that old tin roof.

Now the ninety-year-old barn is being disassembled. It stands, like an aging person undressing in public, stripped of the red siding, with rotting timbers pointing skyward.

The daughter, old herself, saddened by the sight, realizes that memories of a joyous childhood are not so easily destroyed.

Thanks to the new owners, she has hanging in her kitchen an ancient piece of wood bearing the inscription "C J S" in sprawling black letters.

Glancing at the old plaque as she does her daily chores, the daughter often smiles, remembering the barn that would not die and her father who loved it so.

15

We Kept Our Day Jobs

Timothy has told us about your faith and love. He has told us that
you always have pleasant memories of us. I Thessalonians 3:6

There's a big push toward legalizing gambling in our state. Big deal!
We've been legally gambling on Nubbin Ridge for the past forty-five years.
We're in the cattle business.

Webster defines gambling as "to risk something of value on the out-
come of an event." When my husband suggested in 1951 that we should
invest our meager savings (something of value) in a couple of milk cows
whose milk we would sell to Kraft Foods and whose calves we would sell
at the sale barn and use the money to buy more cows, I never once thought
of it as a gamble. Sounded like a real deal to me.

We both had jobs during those years of raising kids and cattle. We
switched to beef cattle when Hubby decided if we had twenty five beef
cows one of us could quit our job. We would be financially secure. It took
ten 500-pound calves to buy a new pickup truck then.

When we reached the magic number of twenty five we realized we would
need at least fifty mama cows to provide for upcoming college costs for
three teenagers. We needed more land on which to run the cattle plus a
barn. We kept our day jobs.

It was about the time we increased our herd to fifty head, mostly Here-
fords, that Hubby thought maybe we should switch to one of the more
exotic breeds; something "with a little ear" as the sale barn man said. That's
when we started investing in Charolais bulls. We kept our day jobs.

Over the years the children left, one by one, as children do, leaving Pa
and me alone. (We had a new grandson who had renamed Hubby). We now
had fifty or sixty sometimes fat and sometimes skinny cows grazing on our
rocky hillsides and I thought we must be approaching Utopia. Wrong! By
now it took forty calves to buy a new pickup truck and we needed new
fences around most of the place. We kept our day jobs.

Now, time has taken its toll. We both stay home. We never reached the
financial security I expected. Cattle prices have sagged, feed costs are sky
high and a nice new pickup truck can be bought with the income from
approximately seventy three head of 500-pound calves.

But you know what?

During the years where else could I have witnessed the awesome sight
of a newborn calf, the fragrance of new-mown hay and experienced a way
of life which soon will have disappeared from the landscape forever?

I wouldn't take "nothin" for the journey. I wouldn't have missed it for
the world.

Autumn Courting

When I found the one I loved I would not let him go 'till I had brought him to my Mother's house. Song of Songs 3:4

It was in the autumn when I met him. He was hitchhiking and I was driving Daddy's maroon-colored 1940 Chevrolet pickup truck with a black stock rack. I stopped to pick him up.

On the bumpy ride into town he managed to ask me out and I managed to accept. We met at Bishop's Drug Store that night, a rainy night, and drove to the county seat to attend the picture show.

Even then I was terribly nearsighted and in the way of young girls I was also terribly vain. My thick eyeglasses were never removed from the case. The movie we saw that Saturday night must have been a comedy. My myopic eyes registered only a blur but I laughed heartily each time my new friend did.

As the evening progressed we recalled meeting seven or eight years earlier at a school bus stop. I was a shy, awkward seventh grader at the time and he was a sophisticated senior.

We continued to see each other in the weeks to come, my new friend and I, much to the chagrin of my parents and I suspect much to his parents disappointment as well. You see, we were not well suited for one another.

He was a hard worker. I had spent most of my life in school or reading library books. The women in his family could cook and sew and clean with the best of them. I could name the four sisters in *Little Women* and the author of the book.

I was unnaturally tall for a girl. He was of average height. I had a little money saved. His pockets were empty at the time.

But somehow, regardless of our differences, regardless of other folks' disapproval of our friendship, on Dec. 22, 1949, we eloped.

Just before Christmas this year, we celebrated our forty-seventh wedding anniversary. In spite of picking up a hitchhiker, failing to listen to my parents and marrying someone who was totally different from me, I can honestly say I believe the marriage is going to last.

'He's Still Real Cute'

I am my lovers and my lover is mine. Song of Songs 6:3

When my husband and I married nearly half a century ago it was for one reason. Our hormones kicked in. In those long ago days when that happened nice girls got married. Thanks to Mama's strict upbringing if I was nothing else I was a nice girl.

Unfortunately, we forgot to check on our other similarities. When the dust settled, we were each a little startled to learn that hubby had always hoped for a life like his parents, living on an Arkansas farm surrounded by as many cattle as possible, while I thought the academic life (perhaps being a perpetual student) would be nice.

He knew how to save money. I knew how to spend it. I longed to travel. He inherited his grandpa Anderson's homing instincts, an old gentleman who spent only two nights away from home in sixty-five years.

But thanks to those same hormones and the fact that we had three little kids in the first seven years of our marriage, kids whom we both adored then and now, our marriage has survived.

In fact, we have learned to settle most of our differences amiably except for the travel thing. I have learned that going for a drive at sunset with my husband means driving in circles around the pasture checking the cattle.

However, hope springs eternal and so when hubby invited me to ride with him to the creek farm to get a round bale of hay recently. I jumped at the chance.

After spraying on a bit of cologne, running a comb through my sparse grey hair, smearing on bright pink lipstick and slipping into a pair of sandals, I settled into the passenger side of the seventy-something blue Chevy pickup with the bale mover on the back. I felt rather glamourous for our little impromptu drive until a glance in the mirror told me I looked more like Lewis Rukeyser than Sharon Stone.

All would have gone well except the area in front of the barn where the bales were stored was a cesspool of cow manure and mud. Hubby suggested that I not only jump out of the truck and open the barn door, but that I fend off the starving cows with a hickory stick until he could spear the bale and pull the truck from the barn. I declined.

Later, as we carefully crept the five or so miles back to the homeplace with the bale balanced precariously on the back of the aging truck, few words were exchanged. No one wore a smiley face. We were not happy campers.

Yesterday in the post office, a former student of mine, an attractive young woman in her forties, asked about my husband's upcoming birthday. When I revealed our ages she smiled, saying, "Yes, but you know, he's still real cute." I had to agree.

On The Shelf

*A cheerful heart is good medicine, but a crushed spirit
dries up the bones. Proverbs 17:22*

Some folks lament their lost youth. I don't. I never knew the pleasure of
resting when I was a kid because I seldom got tired. Now I am tired more
than I am rested. Children have never realized the sheer joy of bending
one's knees (if one can still bend them), and slowly sinking into the soft
comfort of a favorite chair.

Someone asked President Dwight Eisenhour what he intended to do
upon retirement. "I plan to sit in my rocking chair for the first six months,"
Ike replied, "and then I intend to start rocking."

Kids are usually blessed with good digestive organs. They eat anything
and everything with few bad results. They can eat cold chili for breakfast
and their stomach never protests. Aging changes that. One good indicator
that you are reaching the pleasurably period of advanced age is when you
start to belch. Kids never know how good a belch feels. They may hiccup
from time to time but that is nothing in comparison to a deep, straight from
the "innards" belch. That comes with age.

I never see children talking to themselves except in play. Older adults
do it as a way of life. I wander through the labyrinth in the grocery store,
searching for seldom seen items like toothpicks or kitchen matches, and as
I search I talk to myself. Often I meet a person near my age, also searching
and also talking.

My best conversations with myself are in the privacy of my own home.
"Let's see, where did you put the sugar bowl?" I ask myself. "Probably in
the refrigerator," self replies, "As the butter seems to be melting in the
kitchen cabinet where you usually put the sugar."

Human anatomy changes with the years. Children are straight little creatures while most people my age have developed a shelf.

As we eat more food throughout the years and spend less time working
and more time sitting we grow these little shelves. They are usually located
in the abdominal area and are incredibly convenient.

When reading one can rest his magazine or newspaper on the shelf.
One's arms can rest there at church or during meetings. I have even seen
shelves of such magnitude that they could be used as a table to hold a
cheeseburger, fries and a coke.

Someone wrote a book called "Old Age is not for Sissies." True. But it
is not a bad time either, especially when resting comfortably in an easy
chair watching one's shelf grow.

Names Are Important

For every animal of the forest is mine and the
cattle on a thousand hills. Psalm 50:10

I think everything deserves a name. My husband does not. I have a computer with a cow/calf program which I cannot use because our cows have neither names nor numbers.

"The little red heifer's mother must have been in the acorns from the looks of her," my husband observes. I don't know who he is talking about. It seems to me we have several little red heifers.

I only have two cows of my own. The black Brahma cross-bred, with a bobtail and a white calf. I call the cow Roseilita and her calf Juanita. I can tell from looking at a cow what her name should be.

My new cow is a Simbrah. She came from the sale barn, which is a lottery type operation. You pay your money and you never know for sure what you will get.

She is a magnificent cow, dark red, blaze face, and with the floppy ears I like in a cow. I named her Mylanta.

I think Mylanta is a pretty name, regardless of its antacid connotations. When I was a child my favorite paper doll was called Alimony.

Mylanta is not merely a Simbrah, she is a registered Simbrah. When I called her former owner I learned why she was sold at auction. "Why when that heifer was due to calve she prolapsed," the owner informed me. Once a prolapse, always a prolapse, she informed me.

I'm not worried. I like Mylanta. She is bred back to a registered Simbrah bull. I think I will be lucky in this lottery.

It's nice to name pieces of real estate. I call our farm Nubbin Ridge. My dad named the area where we live Nubbin Ridge years ago. His reason: The poor, rocky soil would only grow corn "nubbins" in comparison to the big, corn ears along Yocum Creek where I grew up.

When I was a child the parents of my best friend had a patch of land which they simply called "The Forty." It was flat and located a mile or so from their home. Although they had many more acres folks knew exactly what they meant when they referred to "The Forty."

My sister lives in another state but owns property near us. One piece of land is quite small and borders Yocum Creek. My husband usually identifies to it with the expression, "Your sister's little bottom!" I am working on a new name that would be more appropriate and not quite so graphic.

We need to name things.

Patent Medicines Still Alive

Is not wisdom found among the aged? Does not long
life bring understanding? Job 12:12

I read in last week's *Arkansas Gazette* where a fellow's stomach exploded after he drank a glass of water with a spoonful of soda stirred in. I was devastated. This concoction has always been my favorite remedy for indigestion.

Many of the old remedies are gone, replaced by drugs whose names I cannot pronounce.

I grew up in the age just before "wonder drugs." Mama's cure for a persistent cough, especially at nighttime, was a teaspoonful of sugar laced with a little turpentine.

Scabies, or the itch, or whatever they call it now, was treated with sulphur or boiled pokeberry roots. If one of us children had a temperature, Mama put a cold, wet cloth on his head. If we felt sick at our stomach she dabbed a little camphor on our throat and gave us a rag dipped in camphor to hold to our nose.

Patent medicine, as it was called in those days, could be bought at the local drugstore. Most families kept a supply of Carter's Little Liver Pills on hand for those times when, as Grandpa Stafford put it, "we were feeling dauncy."

If one had a backache there was always Doan's pills and for the young lady who might be suffering from typical young lady complaints there was Lydia E. Pinkham's Vegetable Compound, made especially for women.

Irregularity was treated with an assortment of vile tasting stuff, chief among which was castor oil. There was also Black Draught and if a child happened to have a bad case of worms (which was frequent in those days), she was given a liberal dose of Jayne's Vermafuge.

Life was simpler in those days. If one needed a doctor he came. No one's mama went to work so there was always a comfortable lap to sit in when one was not feeling well.

But it was a scary time as well. Diphtheria killed babies, two of my close friends contacted polio, and rheumatic fever left me with a heart condition which I have carried into adulthood.

I still think baking soda and water are good for indigestion (the man whose stomach exploded had eaten homemade chili, drank two beers and a glass of wine before his internal combustion), and I still sleep with Vicks Vaporub by my bed ready to unstuff a stuffy nose.

However, I am grateful for modern medicine and well trained doctors. It is a great time to be alive!

21

A Piece Of My Heart

*Each has a particular gift from God, one having one kind
and another a different kind. I Cor. 7:7*

They buried the old church today. It was built in 1938 by the men of the congregation after the other church burned.

I can still see Daddy standing in the wagon bed, sweat staining his worn work shirt, urging the team of bay horses on towards the town as they strained to carry a load of Yocum Creek gravel to the church building site on South Springfield Street.

Mama did her part by donating quart jars of thick, yellow cow cream to the Ladies Aid Society for their weekly building fund dinners.

As the years passed the new church became a treasury of memories for each member of the congregation.

I held the sweaty palm of my first beau while sitting in the back pew of the church during Sunday night services.

My husband and I carried each of our three babies in turn down the aisle to be christened. Later we beamed with pride as our little kids wore towels on their heads and became shepherds in the annual Christmas program.

When my brother died suddenly and much too young, that old building held our family, our church family and our wise pastor in its embrace and we were comforted.

Eighteen years ago our only daughter and her friends decorated the church with fresh greenery and dozens of candles along the old chancel rail in preparation for a Christmas wedding.

But it all ended today. The yellow pieces of heavy equipment moved into place and shoved the once-proud structure into the basement below.

Some said it was an eyesore sitting next to the beautiful new church, others said the space it occupied was needed for a parking lot, and others thought it could be dangerous in years to come.

Not being a wise person, I do not know. All I know for sure is that when they buried the church, a piece of my heart went with it.

The Wheels of Progress

For the earth is the Lord's and everything in it. I Cor. 10:26

I've always liked the neighbor's farm. It is eighty or so acres of partly flat, partly hilly, partly wooded and partly cleared land. It lies further up Nubbin Ridge than our place. If one can be technical about such matters, the neighbor's farm lies between Nubbin Ridge and Huckleberry Ridge.

Our neighbor, who had owned the place for the past forty years or so, had made it even more desirable by the way in which he cared for the land.

He had a deep respect for the earth. He cared about the soil, the trees and the water and the wildlife which surrounded his farm.

Trees were trimmed and allowed to grow year after year until giant oaks swayed majestically over the simple two-story frame house and the farm at large.

Springtime brought forth the fragile beauty of dogwood blossoms, masses of them, which greeted the passerby from inside my neighbor's fence.

My neighbor befriended the little wild creatures from the nearby woods. He often placed a pan of food outside his door which attracted a fox and a possum, who soon became regular visitors.

My neighbor died recently leaving his life's work for others to tend. The farm was sold and in place of my gentle neighbor we now have the Wheels of Progress.

Yesterday I saw a pair of yellow bulldozers pushing their way through cedars, hickories, and sumac. I could smell the trees' pungent odor before they were shoved aside and burned.

The sound of the chainsaw is heard over the land as older trees toppled to earth and go to a sawmill.

The Wheels of Progress are making great strides as they transform my neighbor's land into a profitable place. So what if the possum, "who couldn't look for eating, and the fox who couldn't eat for looking," have lost their homes forever. Progress is the name of the game you know.

Somebody's Kid

*I heard the voice of the Lord saying, "Whom shall I send, and
who will go for us?" and I said, "Here am I; send me!" Isaiah 6:8*

I am a retired schoolteacher. I have many children. I carried three of
those children in my body for nine months each. I nurtured the rest of my
children in the classroom for an equal length of time.

After spending seven hours a day, five days a week for thirty six weeks
with a child, they become "yours" in a strange, unexplainable way.

"Yes, Joe was one of my little fifth graders," I say proudly, upon learning that Joe, who now has a receding hair line and a noticeable paunch, has
received some honor. To me, Joe will always be that freckle-faced boy,
sitting in the second seat from the front, who delighted in dusting erasers
and washing chalkboards, but was not above sending a paper airplane aloft
when no one was watching.

Those students who sat in my classroom off and on for the last forty
years are scattered now. Some kept in touch and others did not. When I
hear from them I still say, just as most parents do, "Yes, she is one of my
girls. She was as smart as a whip in school and she still is."

My students were bright, funny, kind, and ambitious. As the years passed
they began to change in one respect and I began to worry.

Our country became more prosperous, and times became easier. It seemed
the young people were more interested in themselves than others. They
were still bright, funny, and kind, but they seemed to become very materi-
alistic.

"If times ever get tough, will these kids be strong enough to survive?" I
sometimes wondered to myself.

Now I know. I have lived long enough to see it. These kids are very
brave and strong.

How do I know? I see them buckling down to fight a war they didn't ask
for and didn't cause. A war not only being fought in the sands of a desert
half a world away, but a war being fought here at home as young mothers
and fathers and husbands and wives cope with the absence of a military
spouse.

I know because some of my students still keep in touch. The one who
used to tease me in accounting class is aboard a mine destroyer in the Per-
sian Gulf. Another who once brought me a Care Bear because he said I
deserved it for putting up with him, is dug deep in a foxhole not far from
the border of Kuwait.

Somewhere in Saudi Arabia, working in a Marine hospital, is a young woman, an anesthesiologist, who long ago sat in my classroom and shared her dreams with me.

This generation too soft? I think not. When I watch television and see the young faces with helmets fastened and gas masks ready, or see a soldier driving a tank along a sandy road in a land which until now had only been known to most through the Bible, or a pilot with a crooked grin and a thumbs up as he takes off for yet another mission, my eyes overflow with tears and I say another prayer.

I believe courage is not the absence of fear, but going ahead in spite of fear. My heart swells with pride as I watch these brave, young Americans, some of them my kids, and each of them somebody's kid, "doing the hard work of freedom."

Trottin' Through Childhood Memories

Pleasant words are a honeycomb, sweet to the soul and
healing to the bones. Proverbs 16:24

I have always worried. Even Sunday morning at church I worry whether the bald spot on my head is adequately covered by my thin, gray hair.

While waiting in the checkout line at Wal-Mart sometimes I wonder if the single black hair which makes its appearance periodically just above my upper lip has quietly resurfaced.

Even as a nine-year-old I was apprehensive about asking classmates to write in my autograph or memory book. What if they failed to write that favorite verse of all times, "Roses are red, violets are blue, sugar is sweet and so are you?" What if they said something really awful?

Sure enough, interspersed between lines from my teacher in which she said I was a "very sweet little girl," and my much older sister declaring she would love me forever as I had been such a good baby, other things were said.

"When you get married and live by a well, wash your feet and change their smell," my niece, who usually shared my bed, said. While Billy Ray, a nice neighbor boy, penned in a bold scrawl, "Red oak leaves, blackjack bark, Green Forest girls are hard to spark. Yours 'til the cows come home!"

Many of my fourth grade friends seemed to have been much aware of our coming adulthood. "When you get married and have twins, don't come to me for safety pins!" Faye G. warned. Robert, in the same vein, wished me luck, wished me joy, and wished me first a baby boy. And when his hair began to curl, he wished me then a baby girl.

But probably the most cavalier attitude was expressed by the boy who wrote, "When I am dead and turnin' rotten, just think of me and keep on trottin'."

Not exactly a Hallmark greeting but sage advice none the less from one little kid to another.

No One Writes Letters Anymore, They Just Call

I have hidden your work in my heart. Psalm 119:11

I miss letters. Real letters from real people which one once found tucked into his mailbox.

My friend, Thelma, age ninety three, writes letters, dozens of letters each week, wonderful descriptive affairs which not only enrich one's life the first time they are read but continue their enrichment with each repeated reading. A telephone call just doesn't do it.

My own children once wrote little notes to me, mostly funny notes which I still cherish. There is the one our son wrote at age eight, after caring for his younger siblings one day while I went into the grocery store. It was a cryptic message, "If you had ten keds (sic) what would you do? Buy a gun and put a bullet in it?"

On her first trip to camp the following message arrived from our ten year old daughter; "I have been very sick. I have had a terrible cough. All of my clothes are dirty. It is scary here at night. Don't worry about me. Love, Alice Gaye."

A couple of poignant letters from another century were found in the attic of an old farmhouse in our neighborhood recently. Both letters were written in the summer of 1899 to a woman named Eliza.

Eliza it seems, was visiting family near Green Forest and her husband, living in northern Missouri wrote to her saying: "Dear Wife, I am just about like I was when you left. Have you got your visit about out? I want you to rite (sic) when you want to come home and I will meet you at Osceola. I got Lillie to rite (sic) this for me. Rite (sic) just as quick as you get this letter. I want to hear from you. Your loving husband, Joseph".

The second letter, also to Eliza, was dated August 4, 1899 and was in an envelope edged in black, which indicated to the recipient that the enclosed letter contained a death message.

"Dear Friend, It is with sorrow that I have to let you know that we layed Joseph away to rest yesterday at six o'clock in the graveyard. He ate dinner with us Wednesday and started up to John's house and his horse backed down that big hill and the buggy, horse and all went off to one side of the bridge with him under them.

They taken him onto John's. He passed away about ten. I could tell you more than I can write. From your friend, A.V."

A woman's sorrow can still be felt upon reading these letters. Could studying a telephone bill have the same results? I think not.

27

The Awful Augusts of Arkansas

*I will send you rain in its season and the ground will yield
its crops and the trees of the field, their fruit. Lev. 26:4*

June bugs are gone, young skunks are showing up as road kill, cicadas sing their nightly courting song and the goldfinch are nesting as thistles go to seed. It is August in the Ozarks.

Cousin Pauline says nature's signs are showing that we can expect an early frost, around September 15. Nights are cool and days are comfortable. What does it mean? Are the awful Augusts of Arkansas a thing of the past?

No air conditioning, no indoor plumbing and no cool spots in those long ago days of late summer.

Mornings were spent on the screened back porch which ran the length of the west side of our sprawling farmhouse. In early August my parents, each holding a dishpan full of freestone peaches, sat on that porch, peeling and canning several bushels of that most delicious of fruits.

Afternoons were spent in Yocum Creek where my siblings and I along with most every other kid in the neighborhood splashed in the icy water. There were dangers of course, snakes and an occasional leech which would fasten with fierce tenacity onto our feet or legs.

Mama, who never accompanied us on these outings, always outlined the dangers in great detail. "And girls," she would say, "Whatever you do, come straight home if any town boys show up at the swimming hole!" Town boys, you see, were skinny-dippers and Mama certainly didn't intend for her girls to see that. Much to our sorrow we never did.

The Stafford swimming hole eventually shrunk to a mud hole after my dad sold the gushing spring above it to the city and its water was used to wash chickens rather than to cool off a bunch of sun-tanned, knobby-kneed, briar-scratched kids on an August afternoon.

Now with air conditioning to cool children, television to watch and an assortment of store bought goodies to drink, who needs a swimming hole?

Take a look at today's headlines and one might decide that perhaps we all do.

The Boys of Yesterday

*They send forth their little ones like a flock and
their children dance. Job 21:11*

They are gone. With them went our energy and most of our brain cells. They are our only grandchildren, ages six and eight. They are Dylan and John-Mark.

We went to the Five Star Theater in Branson, we drove 60 miles a day for five days to basketball camp because our son was the coach, we chased cattle at breakneck speed through tall fescue and taller thistles. We played baseball in the field behind the house, and we survived a near tornado.

"Hurry kids, get into the cellar," I urged, as the warning came over the local radio station. Even the boys' PaPa, who takes great pride in never taking shelter, descended into the damp, dark underside of our house for this one.

John-Mark, a resourceful little fellow, hurried to get a flashlight and a cookie before joining us. Dylan, with the hint of tears in his dark brown eyes, carried his favorite pillow and Baby, a rag doll.

It was a noisy affair, that "nearly" tornado. Hail beat a strong staccato on the metal cellar door, thunder mumbled and bumbled and finally gave a loud ear-splitting belch, as the full fury of the storm hit.

And then the lights went out and with it the argument started between our grandsons over who would hold the flashlight. "I brought it down here, so I get to," John-Mark argued as he flashed the beam on the ceiling, a searchlight looking for spiders.

"But Baby is afraid!" Dylan said in a quivering voice.

But as all things do, the storm passed as did the boys visit and things are quiet once again on our hill. There are few reminders that either the storm or the boys' visit occurred, except for a sagging limb on the oak tree and a baseball glove near the living room door.

And of course there is Clinton, the heeler dog, sitting patiently on his stump, waiting for the boys who tossed a rubber ball to him. The boys of yesterday, but Clinton doesn't know that.

A Brother Remembered

*But while he was still a long way off, his Father saw him and
was filled with compassion for him; he ran to his son, threw
his arms around him and kissed him. Luke 15:20*

Every little girl needs a big brother, especially if he will let her follow after him as my brother did.

We were each born in July but he preceded me by nine years and nineteen days.

My first recollection of my brother was of being pulled in a sled across the snow to grandma's house. I must have been four or five years old at the time.

As the years went by the memories grew. He took me swimming in Yocum Creek and to play in the barn loft where he had built a trapeze. We played football in the front yard on autumn afternoons and checkers by the fire when winter came. He helped me board the school bus and sat by my side on my way to the first scary day of school.

Most everyone in the small town where we lived knew and loved my brother. His large blue eyes, along with a pair of dimples, smiled at the world and seemed to find it good.

My brother was a singer of songs and a writer of tales. He played the piano by ear, sang "Stardust" and other favorite melodies of the day in a lovely baritone and could dance all night.

The story goes that my brother ran away from Mama one day and headed to the country school nearby where all the children were. When Mama arrived huffing and puffing a few minutes later to take him home, the teacher insisted that she let him stay. And Mama did. He was four years old at the time and graduated high school at age sixteen.

Somewhere, in the years to come, the sparkle began to fade from my brother's eyes. I do not know why it happened or exactly when. His classmates, who had voted him class president, most popular and most likely to succeed, eventually married, got steady jobs and settled down. My brother never did.

He was a hard worker but he never stayed with a job long. He roamed the country, searching, always searching. He loved our parents, our other brother and two sisters and me, but while we each found our little niche in the world, he never did. In the end, his dearest possession was a bottle of alcohol.

My brother died in May of 1959, just two months short of his birthday. He was thirty-eight years old.

I will never forget my brother, as neither will anyone who knew him, but each July I remember him even more clearly, and the joys we shared on those long ago days when I dogged his footsteps and he never seemed to mind.

Saying Farewell

A friend loves at all times, and a brother is born
for adversity. Proverbs 17:17

The men of our neighborhood put on their suits and went to town last month to tell Riley good-bye. Riley passed away after spending over forty years of his life in our community. He touched each of our lives. He was past eighty years of age.

Most folks will remember Riley from his uncanny ability to make things grow. His vegetable garden, which was just across the road from his house, was a sight to behold. It seemed that each spring, regardless of the weather, Riley's garden was always bountiful.

And his flowers! They bloomed in profusion in front of his house, along each side of his house and, of course, between rows in the vegetable garden.

Riley was generous. Who in the neighborhood has not been surprised by the put-put of Riley's little three-wheeler, with his faithful dog Snow riding behind, as our neighbor brought us some of his freshly picked strawberries?

Riley had a way with animals. He told us in great confidence that he was feeding a fox and a possum and a stray cat each day from a dish of food placed on the side porch of his house. He did not want too many people to know of the fox and possum for fear the wild creatures would be killed.

Riley and his late wife, Opal, were in their forties when we first knew them. They played with our children, babysat them and reprimanded them when necessary as our little kids grew to adulthood.

Someone once said that in the Ozarks our two best crops are newcomers and paw-paws. Not so with the Jowers family. They fit right in. They were hard workers and good managers and most important of all they were the best of neighbors.

It may be a long time before we see the likes of Riley in New Home community. That's why the men put on their suits, went to town and said good-bye.

31

True Believers

If that is how God clothes the grass of the field, which is here today and tomorrow is thrown into the fire, will he not much more clothe you, Oh you of little faith. Matthew 6:30

Four smooth stones, they rest on the table next to my bed. Dylan, age five, gave them to me. "NeNe" he said, his dark brown eyes gazing into mine, "keep these wocks by your bed and scary tings will go away."

Those little rocks, gathered on our hillside, were given to me in love by my younger grandson. I always smile when my glance falls upon them.

Superstition is sometimes thought to be the exclusive domain of the ignorant and uneducated. Who among us has not practiced it at one time or another?

I spent most of my formative years avoiding stepping on the cracks of the sidewalk. "Step on a crack and you'll break your mother's back," my friends and I cautioned each other as we scampered along the streets of the little town where we attended school.

We made wishes, lots of them, in those days. In addition to the familiar, "Starlight, starbright, first star I see tonight, I wish I may, I wish I might, have the wish I wish tonight," as country children we also wished on loads of hay.

"Load of hay, load of hay, take my wish and go away," we would call in the summertime as the horse-drawn hay wagons filled with the sweet smelling grasses of summer lumbered down the dirt road.

Mama was a believer in the supernatural and for good reason. When she was a little girl, one of sixteen children born to a country store owner in hilly Newton county, Mama had terrible asthma attacks. She had been taken to many doctors but nothing helped. One day the faith doctor came to town.

"I can cure your daughter," he told my grandparents. And cure her he did. This is how it happened.

The little girl and the man walked to the woods behind the child's home. The little girl, my mama, backed up to an enormous tree. The faith doctor nailed a lock of her hair to the tree. He asked her to repeat a certain phrase. He cautioned the child to never reveal the words he told her. The lock of Mama's hair was cut and left hanging to the tree.

When Mama returned to her parents, the faith doctor told them their little girl would have three more asthma attacks; the last one would be so severe they would fear for their daughter's life. After that she would never again have asthma. And so it happened.

What did this mean? Was it the power of suggestion? Did the man have magic powers? Was it blind faith? All I know is that Mama was asthma-free for the rest of her life. Despite the teasing of her five children she never revealed the words the faith doctor had her repeat.

(And I have yet to see a single "scary ting" since Dylan gave me the little flat rocks.)

Last of A Line

My eyes grow weak with sorrow. Psalm 6:7

There is a lonely feeling on our hill. My cousin died yesterday. He was the last of the Stafford men who have lived on Yocum Creek for nearly a century.

Our grandfather came here just after the turn of the century. He traded a grocery store in Missouri for the place. He brought his wife and three children, two boys and a girl, to the old farmhouse, which still stands. Grandpa lived there until his death in 1951.

My Dad, shortly after he married my Mother, bought property adjoining grandpa's place. We all grew up there. Daddy lived there until his death in 1973.

My oldest brother lived on the farm adjoining my parents' place until he passed away eleven months ago, leaving my cousin as the only Stafford man on the creek.

Someday our son plans to return but he is not named Stafford. Neither is my bright, energetic young great-nephew, who in recent weeks has started running cattle along the banks of Yocum Creek.

The hills still watch over our valley, the oak trees still stand, sturdy and strong, and the little creek still wends its way past grazing cattle. But there is sadness that was not here yesterday. My cousin is gone.

He loved the land, as we all do. He mourned the loss of a single tree.

"We may have to cut down the old walnut tree in Grandpa's yard. They tell me it is diseased. What do you think?" he asked each of us anxiously.

Did Grandpa realize what he was doing when he acquired the Yocum Creek farm so many years ago? Was he aware of the way it would tug at the heartstrings of his children and grandchildren, working a magic that would not let them go?

But now they are gone, all the Stafford men who lived on and loved this land.

But maybe not. Maybe there is a great-grandson or two who bear the Stafford name who even now are feeling that mysterious pull to live on the Creek. I hope so. For now that sad, lonely feeling remains.

My cousin is gone.

A Loyal Friend

Each has a particular gift from God, one having one kind
and another a different kind. I Cor. 7:7

He came to us at three months of age, a black bundle of fur, ready to take on the world. His name was True Grit, and we bought him at the Arky Barky kennel just off Cisco Road on Duncan Mountain.

"Do you have any puppies?" I asked, when I called the kennel. "Just one, a Yorkshire Terrier," the owner replied. She went on to say that I could have him at a bargain price because he had an overbite and had been rejected by the pet shop in New York City which had bought his litter mates. A dog destined for a posh life in the Big Apple became a farm dog on a hill farm in Arkansas.

We usually kept his long curly hair clipped short. He chased about the place, riding in the pickup, chasing cattle, swimming in the pond, eating persimmons when they were in season, but at night seeking a friendly lap to curl up in as he dozed.

He was a likeable dog. Lu-Lu, the border collie, who was king of the mountain when he came here, became his best friend. When our daughter would come with her dog, or our son with his two dogs, Grit seemed to be everyone's favorite. He had a special relationship with the UPS driver who would pick him up over near the road and let him ride to the house.

Grit loved to have someone outside with him and I started walking to keep him company. I guess we walked hundreds of miles in the past eleven years. He would bark excitedly when I would put on my old gray sweatshirt and pick up letters to mail in the box a quarter of a mile from the house. He loved to walk.

But two year's ago Grit's heart began to fail. It was a gradual process. Some days I had to carry him home from our walk, but his joy in being outside was undiminished.

The day came when he chose to remain inside. He just couldn't make it any more. Breathing became virtually impossible. In spite of the three types of heart medicine he was taking and a caring doctor, I realized that the time had come to help my loyal friend for the last time.

I took him to the veterinarian and stayed with him as he drifted into a final sleep. I owed him that much. He had stayed with me through good times and bad. Wrapped in his favorite little plaid blanket I brought him home where my husband put him in a special place by the back fence.

He was only a dog, but the love, loyalty, devotion and joy he gave us for eleven years will not be forgotten.

Growing Up Green

Let the little children come to me and do not hinder them, for the Kingdom of Heaven belongs to such as these. Matthew 19:14

I grew up in Arkansas near a small town called Green Forest. My parents were middle-aged at the time of my birth and spent the remainder of their years trying to keep me free of carnal knowledge.

Being a born animal lover, I started chasing roosters away from mama's laying hens at an early age and continued the practice for many years as no one told me why the rooster perched on top of a fat Rhode Island Red hen ever so briefly, leaving the hen to shake herself and the rooster to strut about and crow mightily.

Although we lived on a farm I never saw a bull breed a cow or watched a calf being born or even realized that a steer was a castrated bull, much less that the castration took place behind our barn on those days when mama insisted I stay inside. And I did.

I was about ten-years old when I noticed that my married sister was growing. "What is the matter with Louise's stomach?" I asked Mama. "She used to be skinny and now she has a fat lump right in front."

"Hush, child," Mama said. "If I have told you once I have told you a hundred times, children should be seen and not heard." And so I shushed. But it didn't keep me from wondering.

One day my best girl friend and I were picking gooseberries when a summer shower forced us to seek shelter under a nearby culvert. It was there that we saw the "F" word written in bold black letters on the cement wall. "What does it mean and how do you say it?" I asked my friend who was a couple of years older than I and not quite so green.

Her hasty reply was, "Come on kid, the rain has stopped. We had better get back to pickin' those berries." And we did.

One day, when I was twelve-years old or so, Mama and I were sitting on the cool back porch peeling peaches I said, "Mama, tell me true, where do babies come from?"

"Well, honey," my mother replied softly, "Your cousin Faye told her little boy that babies grow in their mother's stomach and she may be right."

Like most of my friends I grew up in the last years of innocence in our society. And it wasn't bad.

A Ruined Birthday Party

July was even hotter than usual that day in 1939. Yocum Creek, spring fed and usually icy cold, was lukewarm. In Mama's flower garden only the hollyhocks were holding their own. Four-o'clocks and petunias either drooped or rested in exhaustion on the parched earth.

Weather conditions in our North Arkansas Ozarks meant little to me. It was my birthday and I was going to be ten-years old.

My parents were each forty-two years old when I was born and though they had four other children, I was the only one still at home, and some folks said the apple of my parents' eye.

All I know was that each year I was given a lovely birthday party, and this year promised to be the best one of all.

Mama had baked a fine birthday cake decorated with tiny candles from Horton's Variety Store. She had bought six lemons with which she planned to make lemonade and Daddy had stored enough ice in the cellar to make a freezer of ice cream.

But the best part was the guest list. Some of the town kids had been invited to my party. Always before only our nearest neighbor children were guests, but this time Mama had allowed me to invite Bettie Sue, who was just my age and had won the Shirley Temple contest, and Ronnie Lee Deacon, a rather sickly boy who owned all the latest toys. There were other town kids who were planning to make the three mile trip to our farm that day.

The party was to start at one o'clock in the afternoon.

My party clothes were laid out ready to wear. Mama had cleaned the house thoroughly and now there was nothing to do but wait.

It was ten o'clock in the morning when the Posten family drove their team of mules and a rubber-tired wagon into our yard. Mr. Posten cut firewood for Daddy, and they had come to deliver a load. He was accompanied by his wife, Ressie and their son, Luke, who was already ten-years old.

The Postens had moved to our neighborhood a few months earlier, because as Mr. Posten put it, "We jest about starved to death down there at Eros."

The Postens were good workers but they seldom bathed. After each visit to our home Mama had to air the house.

They were also uneducated. Luke had never attended school. He would be a first grader in the fall.

It was only after the wood haulers had unloaded the wood and left, that Daddy told us that he had invited Luke to come back later for my birthday party.

"I can't believe you invited that boy!" Mama scolded. "You knew that some of the town children were coming today. How could you do such a thing?"

I never argued with Daddy, but I knew that I was about to be humiliated beyond redemption. I would be the laughing stock of my town friends. I went out behind the chicken house, sat down under the persimmon tree, and wept.

One o'clock came. The town kids arrived. The girls wore frilly dresses and the boys were dressed in starched white shirts and waist pants. And of course Luke came, barefoot and wearing dirty, faded overalls.

I tried to get some games started such as Blindman's Bluff and Hide the Thimble, but Luke didn't know the rules, so he couldn't play. Besides, some of the kids were already laughing at the way he looked and the way he talked, and I suppose at the way he smelled. Luke climbed high in the big walnut tree and watched the rest of the party from there.

I wish I could say that I defended Luke that day against my friends. I wish I could say that I told Daddy he did the right thing in inviting a poor little boy to my party. I wish I could say that Luke went home feeling good about himself. But I cannot say any of these things.

But something must have happened to me then. I grew up to become a school teacher and a champion of the underdog. I didn't help Luke, but through Daddy's example and the anguish I saw in Luke's eyes, I've been led to help others, and I am glad of that.

Printed May/June, 1993
The Ozark Mountaineer

37

Just An Old Willow Table

June bugs, saturated with over-ripe fruit, rolled like skid row bums under the blackberry bush. Cows left the cool shade of cedar trees to graze and water only after sundown on that long ago summer day on my Daddy's farm.

It was the winding down of Monday, Mama's washday, and my sisters were carrying buckets of the used, gray wash water to pour over zinnias, marigolds, sweet williams and four o'clocks. Daddy, who had been cutting hay all day, was unhitching the horses, a brown gelding named Ted and a little black mare we called Dolly.

We were looking forward to our supper of fried chicken, Mama's buttermilk biscuits, mashed potatoes and gravy, green beans and cold, sweet milk from the cellar.

The year was 1934. I was five-years old, too little to work, but big enough to get in the way of those who were. We lived in the Arkansas Ozarks. Times were hard, and many of our neighbors had moved to California in search of a better life. So far we had managed to stay put, but money was in short supply.

Dorothy, the stock dog, barked sharply. A man with a table strapped to his back was climbing the steep hill leading to our house.

"Well, I declare," Mama said from the kitchen door. "Who is that old man coming up the hill and what in the world is he doing with a table on his back?"

The man, we learned a few minutes later, was from Blue Eye, MO., fifteen miles to the north. He had made the table from willow twigs. I remember thinking that it was about the right size to hold Mama's prized Boston fern.

Our unexpected guest joined us for supper at Daddy's insistence. In those days even surprise guests were offered hospitality. As the man talked and ate and ate and talked we learned that he had lost his job in a saw mill and was trying to eke out a living for his family by making and selling willow tables.

"How much are you asking for the table?" Daddy questioned. The man hesitated. "Six bits," he replied. Daddy pushed his chair away from the empty dining table, stood up, shook the man's hand saying something about how he would like to buy the table but just didn't have the money to spare.

The table maker nodded, thanked Mama for supper, strapped the table on his back and started down the hill in the gathering darkness.

It was then that Louise, my oldest sister, a teenager, burst into tears. Crying, she ran to her room, dug money she had been saving out of the handkerchief box in the dresser drawer and hurried out of the house, calling, "Wait, wait!" to the peddler as she ran.

The willow table was a part of my growing up years and the story behind it as well. My sister Louise taught me a lesson I have never forgotten. There are times in life when it is better to let go of a cherished dream than to watch someone's hope disappear.

Printed June/July, 1995
The Ozark Mountaineer

Good Times

Friendship Is Timeless

*Seeing ye have purified your souls in obeying the truth through the
Spirit unto unfeigned love of the brethren, see that ye love one
another with a pure heart fervently. I Peter 1:22*

There are four of us. We became friends in the ninth grade. We lived
through the Great Depression, World War II and the death of the only president we remembered, F.D.R.

We spent the night at each other's homes, where we stayed awake long
hours talking of boys, what we wanted to be doing in a few years, and what
we hoped to wear to the Junior-Senior banquet someday.

Saturday night was the highlight of our week. We walked around and
around the town square in the little village where we lived, giggling at the
teen-aged boys we knew, who were also walking around the square or loung-
ing against a storefront.

Time passed. High school graduation came and went and the four of us
no longer saw one another on a daily basis. Our lives changed as jobs and
serious romances and college and even marriage occupied our time.

Strangely enough, only one of us left the little village where we grew up
and in later years she too returned.

And now, some fifty years later, the four of us are still friends. We get
together to celebrate birthdays four times a year and it is as though we had
never been apart.

Many things have happened to us in the past half-century. We have received higher education, we have married, (some of us more than once,
due to widowhood or divorce), we have borne children who in their turn
have given us the best of times and the worst of times, and we have learned
to live in a world that has changed in ways we never dreamed possible.

But as we sat around the table celebrating yet another of our birthdays
yesterday, I could not help but think how little we had changed. The one of
us who was always the sweetest was still smiling and speaking to each one
of us with concern despite problems of her own.

The one in our group who has always been so good, so well-behaved
and such a devout Christian is still so. My other friend, a funny, fearless
Irish girl who had entertained us with tales of her escapades in 1943 is just
as gutsy and funny and entertaining today.

To passersby at our birthday table we may have looked like four little
old ladies. Little did they know that in our hearts we were and would always be fourteen-years-old, giggling away another afternoon in springtime.

Everyone Is Good At Something;
Just Find Out What That Something Is

And to one he gave five talents, to another two, and to another one;
to every man according to his several ability; and straightway
took his journey. Matthew 25:15

I still remember when they moved to our neighborhood. I was about ten years old. I remember hearing Daddy telling Mama that some folks from up north had bought the old Shinnley place and that he (meaning the father) was a college professor.

Thoughts of a college professor filled my head for days. In many of the books I checked out from the local library I had read of professors, but I had never seen one. Would he be old? Would he have a mustache? Would he know all there was to know about everything? "But of course he would," I reasoned, "he was a professor, wasn't he?"

One night after the cows were milked and supper dishes put away, Daddy said, "Well, we might as well drive over and see the new neighbors." And we did.

Just as I had expected, the neighbor's house was filled with books. More books than we had in our local library. Shelves of books, stacks of books, and partially read books rested on every flat surface in the house.

In addition to the books, and to the professor, who incidentally had a mustache, and a wife and an adult daughter, there were strange pictures hanging about, pictures which I learned in later years, were painted by famous men. At the time I was intrigued, not by the painter, but by the subject matter. As Mama said later, "Lord a mercy, some of the folks in those pictures were half naked!"

Our new neighbors were kind and generous. They gladly loaned me the first copy of *Wizard of Oz* I had ever seen.

They also used words the meanings of which I did not understand, and seemed knowledgeable on every subject. It wasn't until several days later that I changed my opinion of our intelligent neighbors.

Daddy and I stopped by their house in search of a missing cow. "Well, I did hear a cow mewing sometime in the night," the neighbor's daughter said seriously.

I looked at Daddy as he continued to look at her with a respectful gaze. "Cows don't mew, cats do that," I thought, but taking a page from Daddy's book, said nothing.

"I see some tracks out here along the road," Daddy continued. "Did you see any cows go past your house?"

44

"Well, yes, I did," the daughter replied. "It was a large cow, a boy cow I believe, and it was pink!"

"Daddy," I asked, when we managed to get back to our pickup truck without dissolving in laughter, "how can a college professor's family not know anything about cows?"

"Just remember this, Fay Neen," Daddy said as he started up the motor, "no one knows everything, and most everyone knows quite a bit about something."

When I became a school teacher a decade later, I remembered Daddy's words. It was true. Every child, in every class I ever taught, was good at something. My job was to find out what it was.

God in Wal-Mart?

As water reflects a force, so a man's heart
reflects the man. Proverbs 27:19

I heard it in church Sunday. Not from the preacher. It came from the mouth of a three-year-old with deep blue eyes. "I saw God in Wal-Mart," she confided as she and a half-dozen or so other children sat at the minister's feet listening to the children's sermon.

God in Wal-Mart? As my teenager friends would say, "Cool!" That afternoon, in search of potting soil and God I hurried to Wal-Mart.

Walking from the parking lot into the store I barely missed being struck by a car, a car carrying three women. As I jumped out of the way I saw that none of the trio were wearing smiley faces. I was thankful that hand gestures were not included in their disgust.

"I need eighty pounds of potting soil," I explained to the tall young man working the register in gardening. "I will need assistance in loading it as I have had eye surgery." I handed him my money.

I had thrown the clerk into confusion. He explained that he was the only one working in that department and he didn't know what to do, as his eyes kept darting to the line of people forming behind me.

Next I walked from gardening to the service desk to explain my problem. A young blonde girl suggested I ask an employee who appeared to be in a managerial position. The woman, short with graying hair, exhibited the walking skill of a marathon runner. Breathlessly, I chased after her.

"Oh," she said, "They will be glad to load your potting soil back in gardening." Feeling waves of frustration, I paused for a minute to remember that I was not only looking for potting soil, I was searching for God as well.

Making an effort to speak in a kind voice, I told of the staffing situation in gardening. Without another word the speedy lady called a young boy to close down his register and accompany me on what was by now becoming a familiar walk to gardening.

Quickly, efficiently, and with a warm friendliness, the boy picked up the two forty-pound bags, loaded them into my van, wished me a good day and walked briskly back across the parking lot.

I found potting soil, I thought, as I drove home. But did I find God? Maybe.

Life Goes On, and So Do We

*Pride goes before destruction, a haugnty spirit
before a fall. Proverbs 27:19*

"Life is like an onion; you peel it off one layer at a time and sometimes
you weep," Carl Sandburg said. Some say the tears flow more readily in
the Golden Years.

Social security determines that the golden years begin at sixty-two. AARP
identifies the magic moment as fifty-five. Our mirrors tell us that gravity is
doing strange things to us, sometimes in our third decade.

It is then that we first notice that our hair is often turning gray. Body
parts which once faced the world pert and erect develop noticeable sags.
The horrible drivers license photo taken three years ago suddenly look good.

By the time one is approaching the fifties cosmetic worries are replaced
by nagging suspicions of deteriorating physical conditions. Minds are filled
with facts and numbers.

"What is your cholesterol?", we ask our friends. "Let me tell you about
my HDL and my LDL and my ratio and my blood pressure reading and my
medication," we continue eagerly. Our once stimulating conversation now
sounds like a page from the *New England Journal of Medicine.*

It is about now that husbands begin to consider their wives no longer
lovers but mothers. They even change her name. "Mama," they will ask,
"Is it all right if I eat bacon for breakfast today? Is it on my diet?"

The sixties seem, from personal experience, to be the decade of making
a fool of one's self. First, there is the memory thing. What has happened to
names which were once on the tip of my tongue? Did I swallow them,
never to be regurgitated?

And where did pride go? I recall how tacky I thought Mama looked in
her flannel nightgown, with her hair in rollers, while I, as a young bride,
was reluctant to remove my makeup before going to bed at night.

I knew I had reached an all time low last night, when in the throes of a
sinus attack, I slipped over my nose one of those masks worn to avoid
pollen, and pulled a pink knit stocking cap over my ears when I climbed
into bed.

Heaven help me when I'm seventy.

Helping With Feeding

Wives, submit to your husbands, as to the Lord. Ephesians 5:23

Our sons fed hay when they were at home. My husband would drive the pickup and the boys, with long arms and legs flying, would make quick work of dispensing bales of fescue to the hungry cows.

Later, my husband fed hay alone. He would gear the truck down, leave the motor running, and follow behind the slow moving vehicle as he rhythmically tossed portions of hay to the right and to the left.

Now we are in phase three of hay feeding. I drive the truck while my husband rides in the back cutting the strings that bind, and then separating the bales into edible portions. He gives me instructions. "Just go due east," he says. "Aim for the sycamore tree."

Aiming for the sycamore tree is the least of my worries. I have to drive through a herd of forty or fifty milling cattle, who from their actions, expect to die of starvation within the next thirty minutes. In my little pumpkin yellow truck I am a piece of bark set afloat in a raging ocean of bucking and bawling cows and calves.

After surviving that obstacle course my work becomes routine. I am dressed warmly for my job, wearing a hooded sweatshirt, a fleece-lined denim jacket, a ski mask and insulated gloves. When the cantankerous heater finally warms the tiny cab, I daydream as I creep across the wide expanses of dead grass.

Suddenly my husband's face appears at the pickup window. The expression on his face is not a pretty sight. "I have been hollering at you for the last five minutes," he says. "You lost two bales when you crossed that last draw."

It is only then that I realize that the sycamore tree is far to my right and that if I continue in my present course the line of feeding cattle would extend from south to north, not west to east as directed.

I am not very good at my job but at this period of our lives I seem to be the only help available.

Decisions About Cattle
Are Never Made Lightly

*Moreover, when God gives any man wealth and possessions and
enables him to enjoy then, to accept his lot and be happy in his work,
his is a gift from God. Ecclesiastes 5:19*

The decision to sell cattle is never made lightly. I have known that since
I was a child listening to Daddy and Grandpa discuss the relative merits of
selling the little end of the big cattle or the big end of the little cattle.

Once the decision is made the work is far from over. First the cattle have
to be "got in" as my husband says. Since we run a cow-calf operation, the
calves, who have been weaned months earlier and placed on a pasture we
call the forty (which happens to be forty acres in size), must be corralled.

There is no corral on the forty for two reasons: (1.) Corrals are expensive
to build. (2.) A corral away from a dwelling might encourage would-be
cattle rustlers. The first job is to put together a make-shift corral.

Once the calves are tricked into the corral with feed, the fun starts. Which
calves to sell and which calves to keep? My husband, the big wheel in this
operation, decides. Unlike judgment day, many are called and most are
chosen. One person stands at the gate while others attempt to chase the
cattle designated as unready to sell from the corral without releasing the
big fellows who are McDonald's-bound. It is a time of great stress.

I have been screamed at. I have slid in enormous piles of mushy, green
stinky-stuff, and I have on one or two occasions stalked back to the truck to
sit out the rest of the work in a pout. As I have said, it is a time of stress and
does not bring out one's best qualities.

Loading the cattle on stock trailers can be quite pleasant if the heeler
dog is working right and none of the cattle decide to jump one of the panels
which make up the temporary holding pen.

Then we go to the livestock auction, a place of strong odors, great
camaraderie, cowboys, would be cowboys, farmers, housewives, children,
a fellow who works the ring called a "set-in" man, and the owner of the
world's fastest tongue, the auctioneer.

Once cattle enter the ring, the set-in man starts the bidding, the auctioneer
starts his chant, and Hubby scans the crowd, hoping, praying, that our cattle
sell well.

It is all over in a matter of minutes. Did the cattle make money or lose
money? It all depends on whether feed was bought right, whether the cattle
stayed healthy, and most of all what the sale barn buyers wanted that
particular day.

And you thought playing the horses or casino gambling was risky? Try
raising cattle, my friend.

A Personal List of the Best Things in Life

So then brother, stand firm and hold to the teachings we passed on to you, whether by word of mouth or by letter. II Thessalonians 2:15

I saw him on television. A man standing in a green field, bordered by trees. "Here," the man was saying, "we can have a gambling casino, which will bring money and jobs and prosperity to the land, if you will only vote right!"

Trees, rolling hills, butterflies and wildflowers traded for a gambling casino, big cars, fancy restaurants and luxury hotels? No way!

My friend gave me a refrigerator magnet. A magnet which, with the message, "The best things in life are not things," set me thinking.

My personal list of best things includes the following: A baby's smile; sitting beneath a giant oak tree on a September morning; the song of a mocking bird at nightfall; hearing the doctor's words, "We got it all,"; the softness of a kitten's fur; total devotion in the eyes of my dog; warm arms and a goodnight kiss from a grandchild; the words, "Hello, Mother!" when I pick up the phone; friends who stay around during the bad times; the spine-tingling cry of a pack of coyotes; bluebirds; someone saying, "You made a difference," church on Sunday morning; childhood memories; the smell of sun-dried sheets; swinging bridges; and surprise lilies popping through the brown grass of August.

The list goes on.

As parents and grandparents, in this age of materialism, perhaps we should teach children and grandchildren that the best things in life are free.

How do we teach? "Impress them on your children. Talk about them when you sit at home and when you walk along the road, when you lie down and when you get up."

Moses' teaching ideas could work today.

Attached to Old Trailer

*He who guards his mouth and his tongue keeps himself
from calamity. Proverbs 21:23*

Many years ago, when we were even poorer than we are now, we decided to buy a horse trailer. All three of the children had a horse and riding their horses to the local showdeos and other horsey events was a problem.

We drove down below Harrison one day and bought a rather nondescript horse trailer in fair condition, which we had heard advertised over a Harrison radio station.

The years went by. The three children grew up and left home to pursue their own private dreams. My husband sold their horses, a big buckskin named Smokey, a palomino Shetland, and the meanest little Welsh pony in Arkansas, who our youngest son called "Blacky".

The only reminder of those days was the horse trailer, which by now was even more nondescript and in poor condition. When we built our house twenty years ago, my husband pumped up the tires on the horse trailer and moved it with us, parking it on the hill behind the new house between a post oak and a persimmon tree. It was never used.

"When are you going to get rid of that trailer?" I would complain at least once a year. "That thing has a good axle in it," was my husband's evasive reply. Time continued to take its toll on the trailer, breaking the rack and rotting the tires, providing a perfect home for an assortment of skunks and squirrels.

Last spring when our neighbor and his father-in-law came to our house to borrow a tractor, an opportunity presented itself which I could not resist. "What about that old trailer sitting up there?" my neighbor's father-in-law asked. He was the first person to show any interest in the eyesore for twenty years. "You can have the trailer if you want it," I replied, smiling sweetly.

The visitor took me up on the offer. My husband wasn't home at the time. I was feeling pretty smug until about thirty minutes later when my husband's pickup truck appeared.

"Who'd you sell the old trailer to?" Hubby asked. "I met someone towing it down the road but I couldn't see who it was."

"I didn't sell it, I gave it away," I hesitantly replied.

"Gave it away? What do you mean, gave it away?" my husband asked. "Why the axle alone in that thing was worth no telling how much."

I kept my mouth shut. Sometimes it's better that way.

Men Know How To Do It Right

There is a time for everything, and a season for every activity under Heaven: a time to weep and a time to laugh, a time to mourn and a time to dance. Ecclesiastes 3:4

When is a woman old? When my grandmother Villines turned fifty she laid down the broom, took off her apron, tied a kerchief around her head, sat down in the rocking chair beside the fireplace, lit a corn cob pipe and never again concerned herself with housework or personal appearance. She was old.

Women are not allowed to get old these days. Watch a talk show, read a women's magazine, learn about dieting, coloring hair, getting a hobby, stretching the mind, running a marathon.

"She's not getting older, she's getting better," we read in a caption beneath a picture of a woman with the body of a sixteen-year-old and the face of a twenty-year-old, whom we are told is actually sixty plus, but just happens to be wearing the right brand of hair color.

There was a time when reaching a certain age meant women no longer had to worry about babies. Not so anymore. With hormone replacement therapy and artificial insemination one can give birth at any age. "Men can father children in old age, why not allow women the same privilege?" is one argument.

Privilege? Get real. With diarrhea, colic and sleepless nights, mother and child could be in diapers at the same time. Or an absent-minded mother could put the poor little baby down for a nap and forget where she put her.

Men seem to have no identity crisis on the age thing. When they reach the late fifties or so, they put their work aside. Then with pot bellies jiggling, and wisps of gray hair waving in the breeze, they amble off to the local coffee shop.

It is here that they stretch their minds with stimulating conversation. "How about that football team?" one says as he hunches over a cup of steaming black coffee.

"Right! How about that team?" his friend replies with a nod and a smile. Both men then gaze contentedly into space. Conversation ended.

Men know how to do it right.

The Day I Killed My Cat

*Look at the birds of the air; they do not sow or reap or store away in
barns, and yet your heavenly Father feeds them. Are you not much more
valuable than they? Matthew 6:26*

It happened Saturday. I was driving the car into the carport when Eureka,
the front porch cat, (who had moved to the carport for the summer), was
resting near the door.

Just as I drove into the carport three things happened: (1) Lucy, the
heeler dog, ran across the yard to chase Eureka, (2) The cat disappeared
from view, (3) I felt the car roll over something solid. I was horrified. Had
I hit my cat?

After a long moment I slowly climbed from the car and looked about.
No sign of my lovely gray and white cat. I called, "Kitty? Kitty?" No reply.

I took the final step and looked under the car. There she was, stretched
out full length. Her head appeared to be near a front tire, but I was afraid to
look closer. The crushed skull of my sweet cat would not be a pretty sight.

I was home alone, and distraught beyond measure. I wished my husband
were there. I tried to call my son. No one home. I called my sister-in-law.
No one home. I paced the floor, wringing my hands in remorse.

If only I had driven more slowly. If only I had not scolded my cat for all
those times she had left little cat tracks on the freshly washed car. If only, if
only.

I looked at the mantel. There sat the exact stone likeness of my cat. A
dear friend had made it for me several years ago. The tears started to fall,
even as I was telling myself that other cats in the animal shelter were now
awaiting a home such as mine. But I didn't want another cat. I wanted
Eureka.

As I grieved, I recalled a book on courage I had read recently. Bravely,
I straightened my shoulders and marched outside to remove the body of
Eureka from beneath the car.

I knelt down, reached as far under the car as I could, and slowly my
fingers touched Eureka's warm, soft fur. Just as slowly, the cat raised her
head and meowed softly.

Joy of all joys, Eureka was fine! The car had run over a corner of a
heavy doormat. I hugged the cat and cuddled her and promised that never
again would I say unkind things to her. Eureka purred softly and nestled
against my shoulder.

Seasons of the Soul

Cemetery Reflections

I am not saying this because I am in need, for I have learned to be content whatever the circumstances. Philippians 4:11

As I write on this Memorial Day, (we used to call it Decoration Day) I am sitting alone in New Home Cemetery.

New Home is part of my past, my present and my future. As a child I played here, as my parents' home was less than a quarter of a mile away. When I had one of my frequent "bunking" parties, I often brought my friends here for entertainment. We would read names on headstones, note the graves of children and as darkness fell, hurry home for some of mama's popcorn, home-made grape juice and fudge.

Today I wait, one of a committee, hoping to receive donations for cemetery upkeep. The quietness is broken by passing automobiles. The largest bluebird I have ever seen perches on a nearby headstone, while a cardinal hen chirps anxiously in the hickory tree above my head.

Yocum Creek, a twisting trail of gleaming silver in the sunlight, races northward in the valley below.

It is an old cemetery, as is the abandoned school house which rests in its midst. Artificial flowers, of such brilliance, that, a pair of monarch butterflies pause for a moment, decorate the graves.

I wonder, as the living have wondered about the dead since time unending, about those who rest here. Tombstones date back to the middle of the last century. Many died before the automobile was invented. Were they happier in those quiet, slower days? Or was it a sadder time when pneumonia and diphtheria claimed more lives and little medical help was available?

Someday, I too will rest here. Will someone sit here, even as I now do, wondering about a woman who died before she ever had an opportunity to fly to the moon?

But perhaps I have known even sweeter pleasures than a voyage through space. I will have heard a robin sing, clear-throated in the dawn. I will have seen an apple tree, clothed like a bride, in white. I will have seen small wild creatures kick up a glittering dust on a snowy morning.

Which is the best, an automobile trip, a space flight, or the simple everyday happenings we so often ignore? All are equally good.

But as Mama used to say, "Bloom where you are planted." Slow down and enjoy life wherever you are because in spite of all we do, life goes on.

No One Ever Told Me

The Lord is far from the wicked, but he hears the prayers
of the righteous. Proverbs 15:29

No one ever told me that the day I gave birth to my first child my world would be changed forever.

I thought, until that late December afternoon in 1950 in a hospital bed in a northern California hospital, that I understood love.

Hadn't I always loved and honored my parents? Didn't my pulse quicken when my young husband of a year entered the room, and didn't joy fill my heart?

But the fierceness, almost primitive love I felt for that seven pound two ounce squirming bundle of humanity placed by my side was almost frightening in its intensity. No one had ever told me.

I became a mother twice more in the next six years. Mentally, if not physically, I drew a circle around my babies. I would, I silently vowed, not only love these children with my very being, I would protect them with my own life if necessary. No one ever told me.

Those years were good years. Their father and I taught our children to work hard and to play fair. Sometimes there were disagreements but always there was love and the children flourished.

But then, one day, that firstborn child, the child whose birth opened my heart to the raw, powerful maternal love for the first time, left home. He was seventeen years old and college bound.

We felt great pride in his accomplishments but there was now a tear in the protective circle I had drawn. No one had ever told me.

Now all three are gone, have been for many years. I can no longer keep them safe, protect them from disappointment.

That is why, each morning, when I awaken, I pray. Pray for each of those children who, despite their ages, are still my babies.

And God, in his amazing wisdom, understands and widens the circle.

No one ever told me.

The Old Mothers

*A new commandment I give you; Love one another, as I have
loved you, so you must love one another. John 13:34*

"What is it like to have a baby?" I asked two old mothers the day I
became a bride.

"Law, child, you will find out soon enough," they replied.

Eleven months later writhing, groaning, pushing and finally crying out
for my own mother, I found out. I became the mother of a baby boy.

I liked mothering. Babies were soft and cuddly and gurgled with
happiness most of the time. Another baby boy arrived in a couple of years,
and three years later a little girl was born.

"I really like this," I told the old mothers. "My children are fun to play
with, quick to learn and respect my wishes most of the time."

"What you are doing now is the easy part," the old mothers said. "Now
they stumble over your toes. Later they will tread on your heart."

Soon the teen years came and it was as the old mothers had said. It was
a time of much cutting. Cutting words were flung about loudly and
eventually came the cutting of the apron strings. And then the children
were gone.

"Well, it is over," I told the old mothers. "The children have grown up
and have left to live lives of their own. Now I shall return to being the
person I was before," I said.

"No," said the old mothers. "Once a child is born to a woman she can
never be as she was before. That person is gone forever."

"Why, then," I cried, "would anyone ever want to become a mother? It
is the worst pain one can endure physically and emotionally. And now you
tell me that I have lost my old carefree self forever?"

"Because," the old mothers carefully explained, "it is only through
mothering that God gives us the gift. The gift of unconditional love for
another human being. A gift which will be carried in your heart to the grave
and some say beyond. It is a love so strong that mothers, animal mothers
and human mothers, not only live for their children but are willing to die
for them as well."

A Mother's Gift

*Can a Mother forget the child at her breast and have no
compassion on the child she has borne? Isaiah 49:15*

A wise person once said, "No matter how old a mother is she watches her middle-aged children for signs of improvement." It's the truth.

My aunt complained about her daughter's actions, "I'll swan, sometimes I don't think that child will ever learn!" My aunt was ninety-two at the time and "that child" was seventy-four.

Mama died when I was thirty-seven years old but as long as her health permitted she was trying to get me "straightened out," literally. "Honey, straighten your shoulders when you walk. Even though you are tall you musn't slump," Mama admonished me when I was ten-years old and continued doing so even when I became the mother of three children of my own.

And now, God forgive me, at age sixty-five, I sound exactly like Mama. To my first born, a six foot three inch forty-four year old land surveyor I find myself saying, "Now son, are you brushing your teeth? Remember what I have always said. If you lose your teeth you can't eat and if you can't eat you die!"

As if that isn't bad enough, I have carried home several different types of toothpaste from Wal-Mart and insisted that my son try them.

Son number two, at age forty-two, is an unmarried basketball coach. He lives alone in a one bedroom apartment and he is not Suzy Homemaker. "Son, if you would clean up this place you would be surprised how cute it would be," I say, as I empty trash, sweep, dust and do laundry. As if that isn't enough I've been known to replace a *Playboy* magazine with some devotional material and place a few of Aunt Chloe's crocheted doilies about.

My daughter, age thirty-nine and the mother of two, keeps house better than I ever have, and has beautiful straight, white teeth. "But," as I tell her, "you'd better watch those little boys. Although they are real sweet now, you can't be too careful, they could get in trouble before you know it. Beware of the teen years," I warn, shaking my head.

But my children, my middle-aged children, are wiser that I have ever been. Instead of arguing with me they each one nod his or her head in agreement, smile, pat me on the shoulder and say, "Yes, Mother," even as they continue doing as they please.

On this Mother's Day, all I can say is, "Thank God for good children, children who can love and tolerate an often imperfect mother."

Spring, Beautiful Spring

I lift up my eyes to the hills-where does my help come from? My help comes from the Lord, the Maker of heaven and earth. Psalm 121:1-2

Spring approaches our farm stealthily as a cat stalks a bird. Quiescently she moves across the fescue field, greening each blade of grass as she comes.

But much as an exuberant child in a game of hide and seek, a dogwood tree on the Stafford hill to the east of us, or a wild plum in the Mitchell woods to the west will burst into bloom overnight, as though shouting, "I am here, I am here!"

The bluebirds and sparrows have renewed their yearly battle over who gets to live in the bluebird boxes along the yard fence. Eureka, the front porch cat, who has only climbed out of her afghan lined basket to eat her daily rations of Kit and Kaboodle now stays out all night.

Once again the phone calls have started, and we appreciate each one of them. "I am not sure, but I think you all might have some cattle out. I saw them along the road as I was going into town," the caller says. Usually it is our cattle and if it is we can count on it being part of the yearling herd. Yearlings will scarcely leave the feeder all winter, but come the first warm day they become vagabonds.

Caught up in the blush and beauty of the season, my husband and I feel bursts of energy as we plan our days work. "I think the first thing that I will do this morning is to fix the fence where those yearlings have been getting out, and then I will haul a few more round bales and then sow some grass seed later today if the wind doesn't get too high," my husband says as he slips on his cowboy boots.

Not to be outdone, and feeling a little frisky myself, I reply, "Well, as soon as I wash the breakfast dishes I plan to rake the yard, dig up a couple of flower beds and paint the porch swing."

Much sooner than we had expected, we find ourselves back in the house, sipping cold drinks, totally exhausted with most of our work awaiting us. I am sure my back will never be the same and my husband says his arthritis has kicked in.

I can't help thinking that the only sap that arose this morning was two old ones, my husband and I, who should have known that answering the siren call of spring in ones sixties is a little different from greeting springtime as a young person. But it is still a fragrant, beautiful, promising time of year.

61

Valentine Wishes

Do not be anxious about anything, but in everything, by prayer and petition, with thanksgiving. Present your requests to God and the peace of God, which transcends all understanding, will guard your hearts and your minds in Christ Jesus. Philippians 4: 6-7

To each of my loyal readers, be you few or many, a valentine wish from my heart to your heart would be that the year we are just beginning would be a slower one. A year when no one would have to say, "Gee, I would like to spend more time with my kids or my parents or my hobby or just to smell the roses, but I'm just s-o-o busy."

I have said it. Haven't you? And at what are we so busy? We live in a world of microwave ovens, fax machines, fast food establishments, automatic washer, dryer and dishwasher; all designed to save time. So why are we so much busier than previous generations?

Could it be a matter of choices? There are more and more choices each year, each day even. Life is not simple. There is also the matter of personal choices. Often we are busy because we want too much.

A friend I have know most of my life has a serenity about her, an inner peace which I have sometimes coveted. She is relaxed and seemingly content although her material possessions are few. I once heard a mutual friend remark about her, "You know, she can get as excited and be as content over a geranium growing in a coffee can as most people can over a new car!"

And so, dear Valentine, despite the world of do more, be more and get more, I wish for each of you and for myself as well, a realization of the truly worthwhile things in life and the ability to enjoy each moment of our lives.

Or, as I heard it expressed so well recently, "People now-a-days don't know how to stop." May you learn to stop. It could prove beneficial to your heart.

The Intruders

Do not forget to entertain strangers, for by so doing some people have entertained angels without knowing it. Hebrews 13:2

It happened in a shed in winter nearly two thousand years ago. Could it happen now, or does it, over and over again?

The temperature was 23 degrees, but a north wind gave the feeling of it being much colder. Mummy-like I struggled toward the barn, wrapped in two layers of clothing and a red ski mask. Although it was not full morning I knew the barn cats were waiting impatiently for their rations.

The heeler dogs, Lucy and Clinton, proved true to their name as they vied for positions near my boot clad feet. It was a normal morning, until I pushed aside the barn door and realized something was amiss.

It was the cats, three of them, who usually wound themselves around my legs, meowing eagerly, who this morning were resting peacefully in the hay, solemnly watching the barn's newest occupants. For there, in the far corner, where the summer's hay was stacked, stood a man with a beard, a girl in her teens and a baby, apparently new-born, wrapped in an old shawl and snuggled into the fragrant fescue.

There was a feeling of peace in the barn that morning, a warmth and a strange light but I didn't linger.

Strangers on one's property are not to be tolerated, even in a corner of the barn. Without uttering a sound I hurried back toward my house, noticing even in my haste a star, a large star which seemed to be hovering over the barn.

Should I wake my husband to this yet another problem? Or would it be better to simply call Sheriff Lonnie? Those strangers might be armed and dangerous. The sleeping baby could be just a ploy.

Or, heaven help us, they could be people who spoke a foreign language or had skin darker than mine. But even as those thoughts rushed through my mind, I longed to return to the warmth, the light and love I felt there.

But when I did retrace my steps, without calling either my husband or the sheriff, the intruders were gone, leaving not a trace but for a thought that keeps coming back to me, time and time again.

Maybe, just maybe, the Christ child comes in many forms, in many ways, on many days of our lives, but in our hurry and anxiety we fail to recognize Him.

Although this is not a true story, don't you think it could have happened that way?

Valentine's Day: 1939

At the time Jesus said, "I praise you, Father, Lord of heaven and earth, because you have hidden these things from the wise and learned, and revealed them to little children. Matthew 11:25

In those February days of 1939, as the Great Depression seemed not quite so harsh and the clouds of World War II were still hidden, the children of Miss Ella Mae Shibley's fourth grade class at Green Forest Grade School were thinking of only one thing, Valentine's Day. I know. I was one of those students.

We bought our Valentine cards at Horton's Variety Store, a forerunner of today's Horton's Five & Dime Cafe in Berryville. Some of us bought packets of 20 valentines which included special cards for a teacher and a sweetheart.

Others chose the slightly smaller penny cards bearing pictures of cowboys and firemen. More creative classmates made original creations with red construction paper, white doilies and flour paste.

Valentine's Day at school was a wonderfully exciting time except for that year in 1939. That was the year we had Helen in our class.

Helen, you see, was a handicapped child, the first one most of us had ever encountered. In today's educational system, Helen would be classified "learning disabled" and receive special care. Not in 1939. We just knew that she was different from us and therefore unacceptable.

I still recall the cruelty on the playground, the teasing, the laughter and most of all Helen's frustration. Sometimes she would cry, sometimes she would yell angrily at her tormentors, and often she would threaten, "I'll tell the teacher!"

I think the thought of our beloved Miss Shibley knowing that I had been unkind was the only thing that kept me from joining in the teasing. "Helen, you won't tell on me, will you?" I would whisper and she never did.

Through a short autumn and a long winter we spent our days with Helen but never accepted her. No one wanted to be her seatmate or to call out, "Red Rover, Red Rover, let Helen come over," in our recess play.

Finally the long awaited Valentine's Day arrived. We struggled to school carrying our precious burdens, valentines chosen and carefully addressed to our special friends.

Miss Shibley had decorated a hat box from Seitz Mercantile in red and white crepe paper, with a big slit across the lid, where we deposited our valentines to be distributed later in the day.

It was a long, long day, longer than usual as we waited for the big moment. Would we receive a special sweetheart Valentine from the one we were "stuck on" as we called it, or perhaps from the new girl, Marjorie, whom everyone wanted to be friends with?

Finally the magic moment arrived. The top came off the box and the heart shaped cards were delivered. Soon thereafter we made an amazing discovery. I think each child in that room received a card from Helen with the following words laboriously printed across the bottom: "Love, from Helen."

I am sure I did not recognize it then but I know it now. Helen had the biggest heart in that fourth grade class.

And God gave it to her.

Prelude to Spring

And they were calling to one another: Holy, holy, holy is the Lord Almighty; the whole earth is full of his glory. Isaiah 6:3

This year it was the eagles and it started in February. Seeing those big birds perched in the sycamore tree by the pond, and watching them swoop into the cow pasture to pick up tantalizing tidbits of chicken litter, it crossed my mind that spring would come again and perhaps soon.

Next came the bluebirds. Unlike our proud scavenger visitors, they were checking out available housing in our neighborhood. After repeated discussions and numerous inspections, mama and papa bluebird settled on an unpainted nesting box on the west fence.

Greening of dormant fescue came next. Fortified by a generous dose of the aforementioned chicken litter, the grass started growing with the fescue covered hills resembling that of a scraggly first beard on the face of a gangly youth.

And then yesterday morning, the first flowers appeared, bringing not only a touch of color to the landscape, but fond memories of the place of origin of the plants themselves.

The japonica came from an old house place located on a farm adjoining ours. According to my calculations, a pioneer woman probably planted the original bush prior to the turn of the century. A woman, perhaps much like myself, who hungered for a patch of color following the drab days of winter.

Women have been sharing flower cuttings with each other for as long as I can remember, and much longer than that I am sure. The green spikes of iris in the corner of my yard remind me of Thelma, who like all true flower lovers gave them to me several years with the admonition, "Now, don't thank me, or they won't grow!"

So as I write this, spring hasn't officially arrived, but her glorious prelude is a special blessing for which I am grateful.

A Hundred Years of Christmas

Follow the way of love and eagerly desire spiritual gifts, especially the gift of prophecy. I Corinthians 14:1

When our grandsons were small, choosing a suitable Christmas gift was no problem. One year we gave John-Mark a rocking horse, the year he was three. My son-in-law, bless his heart, captured for all posterity, on video, me, lanky legs and gray hair flying, astride that pony, teaching John-Mark to ride.

Now gift buying for the boys is a different story. What they want I have not only never heard of, but probably couldn't afford it if I had. There is something called Nintendo 64 which costs mega bucks and is non-existent on most store shelves or so Katie Curic says on the Today Show.

My own children asked for a basketball, toy guns and holster, tiny farm animals and a Barbie doll. As they grew older, they wanted clothes, not name brand stuff but coveralls and jeans in which to do barn chores, books, sweaters and boots.

In my childhood days, the Depression years of the thirties, I was delighted to receive a Betsy Wetsy doll dressed in clothes Mama had made while I slept. There was even a tiny doll quilt on the year I received Betsy Wetsy's wicker buggy.

At Green Forest grade school we decorated our tree with foil saved from cigarette packages which we used to cover the cardboard star for the top. We made red and green chains by coloring and cutting strips of a "Fifty-Fifty" or "Big Chief" tablet.

We drew names for gift exchange with most gifts costing no more than a quarter. (A hamburger cost a nickel and a mixed malt a dime).

My mother marveled at the affluence of my childhood. She described Christmas in her parents' home in Newton County, just before the turn of the century, as a shooting of pistols or rifles to mark the great day and a stocking holding an orange or an apple with a few sticks of peppermint candy.

In reply to my questions about the disappointment the children must have felt on such a sparse Christmas, Mama would always reply, "Well, we didn't expect much and we didn't get much, but we were tickled to death with what we got."

How do we teach that concept to the children of today?

Mr. and Mrs. Santa Claus

He satisfies my desire with good things, so that my youth is
renewed like the eagles. Psalm 103:5

They not only looked like Mr. and Mrs. Santa Claus. Their personalities
were perfect as well.

Although most of the neighbors called them by their first names, Maggie
and Charlie, Mama said that was rude for children and insisted we say,
"Mr. and Mrs. Frazier."

As a child I always recognized that my good friends, especially Mr.
Frazier, were different from most adults in my life. The Fraziers always
had time to play.

It mattered not how often I came calling, nor how busy Mr. and Mrs.
Frazier were, they would stop, bring out the checkerboard or the newest
jigsaw puzzle and we would play.

Also, there was a swing hanging from one of two giant cedar trees in the
front yard in which visiting children could swing.

In later years one could see Mr. Frazier, thick gray hair blowing, enjoying
the swing he had built long ago for his own six children, as well as others.

As a young adult it dawned on me that a trouble free life was not what
put the perpetual smile on Mr. Frazier's face. There had been sorrow, often
and deep, in the lives of my neighbors. Two daughters died at early ages
and a grandson was born blind.

Eventually old age and ill health took its toll on my friends, but still they
kept smiling, always delighting in small things.

As each Christmas season approaches and I tell myself that decorating
a tree is too much trouble now that our children have started their own
family traditions, I remember the Fraziers and change my mind.

In my mind's eye I still can see it, the lighted cedar tree brightening the
window panes of the little log house, covered with brick siding, in which
our neighbors lived. Even with just the two of them, they celebrated each
Christmas with the simple joy of children.

And so, once again, I carry the tree ornaments from the closet and trim
my own tree, feeling grateful to have lived close by and learned so much
from Mr. and Mrs. Santa Claus.

A September Walk

I will lift up my eyes to the hills - where does my help come from?
My help comes from the Lord, the Maker of heaven and earth.
Psalm 121:1-2

Yesterday, with its crispness that only late September can bring, was a perfect day for a walk. Not just any walk. It was the perfect day to take the walk that had been in the back of my mind all summer, a walk across Yocum Creek, then over the bluff and finally to the top of the big hill.

The weather was so nice my husband, reluctant walker that he is, agreed to accompany me. Of course, he did drive the little pickup right up to the water's edge before putting his cowboy boots to the ground.

The creek was shallow, icy cold, and less than knee deep. I brought along an old pair of shoes for the crossing; my husband scoffed, refused to remove his boots, and splashed boldly across. Only later did he mention that his socks were wet.

The route we chose is known as Buzzard Roost Hollow, a deep ravine opening out near the creek. In the midst of ferns, hickories, tiny blue flowers, and the earthy odor of decaying leaves we found the remains of an ancient cookstove. Where had the stove come from, we wondered, as we walked. Had it washed down during a hard rain? What about the woman who once cooked on it? The stove was probably a prized possession seventy-five years ago.

For persons the age of my husband and I, climbing a steep hill is not easy. In fact, when climbing something as steep as that hill cleats would have been nice. We each carried a walking stick, our one concession to advancing years.

My stick, which I bought as a dog training tool, had proved of little benefit in dog training, but is fine for walking. It is made of sweet chestnut wood and weighs about half what a hickory of the same size would weigh. My husband, traditionalist that he is, carried the hickory stick he uses to work cattle.

As we neared the top, I began hearing a steady, "thump, thump, thump," pounding in my ears. Was it a cattle stampede, I wondered, as I huffed and puffed onward, or a run-away train? It wasn't until we stopped that the noise subsided and I realized it was my pounding heart.

As we sat side by side on the grass covered ledge catching our breath and admiring the panoramic view below. I gasped to my husband, "You know, we may be over the hill but at least we are not under it yet."

School Days

In your teaching show integrity, seriousness and
soundness of speech. Titus 2:7

Sixty-one years ago this month, I walked down the hall of Green Forest Elementary school for the first time. My brother, age 15, had lifted me onto the school bus and sat beside me on the four-mile ride to town.

When we climbed off the bus he pointed to the building where I was to go, trotted across the road to join his friends, and I was on my own.

As I moved slowly down what seemed like a very long hall, I remember glancing at each of the eight doors wondering in which room I belonged. It was grade one and I was six-years old.

That morning, in that old brick building, started a love affair between me and the public schools which has lasted to this day.

I liked Mrs. Swor, my teacher. I liked my classmates, my new lunch box, the exact placement of the chairs and desks, the sand table in the corner, the blue-backed primer Mama had bought for me at Mrs. Stacy's bookstore on the square and from which I learned to read, and the old water pump standing in the school yard from which we could get fresh drinks of water.

I liked my clothes, five new cotton dresses with matching panties, which Mama had made, my lunch of home-made bread and ham sandwiches, and my school supplies, a Fifty-Fifty tablet and three lead pencils sharpened by Daddy with his pocket knife.

Fourteen years later, at the age of twenty-two, I found myself entering my first classroom as a teacher, not a student.

The school, Farewell Elementary, was located several miles east of town on a dirt road. There was a wood stove for heat and outdoor toilets, but I was excited and happy. After a childhood of playing school I was at last getting to be a real teacher.

I didn't have a clue how to teach thirty-six students in grades four, five and six under my guidance, but I remembered it as one of the best years of my life. The older students helped the younger, parents were supportive, and I played tag and blindman's bluff with my students at recess.

And now, each autumn, as the monarch butterflies drift southward, the persimmons tinge with color and the yellow buses run, I remember school and my heart gladdens.

I hope that each first grader and each beginning teacher receive the joy and satisfaction that I found once upon a time in the autumn of 1935.

Yesterday's Summers

Be prepared in season and out of season; correct, rebuke and encourage - with great patience and careful instruction. 2 Timothy 4:26

Were they really hotter, those summers of my childhood? Nobody I knew had a thermometer so there is no way to tell.

We had no electricity on our farm, no running water, and no fans, except for the one made of cardboard bearing a colorful advertisement for Putnam Fadeless Dyes and Tints.

Mama and Daddy spent the long days of August preparing for winter. Daddy stored hay, corn, and wheat in the barn while Mama canned tomatoes, grape juice, green beans, relishes, jellies, blackberries, apples, and peaches and stored them in the cellar.

Our house had grown quite large by the time I arrived in July, 1929, creating a mid-life crisis for a couple who had already parented four children and buried two.

As the babies had appeared, new rooms were added, tucked into odd angles on the original three room structure. The grand finale was a large porch, or veranda, as one might call it, snaking around the south and east sides of the old white house.

As the scalding heat of July drifted into the humid languorous stupor of August, even the houses' high ceilings, numerous windows and outside doors were not enough to cool down our sweating bodies enough for sleep.

That's when mattresses were carried to the front porch. About the time fireflies came out, four-o-clocks smelled their sweetest and a sharp eye could spot the sign of dog days in the sky, we fell asleep.

At least twice each summer, my Aunt Jessie and Uncle Harry would come out from town about supper time with a tow sack of ice bought from Mr. Seiniker, the ice man. Mama would carry up a pitcher of cream from the cellar, add a lot of sugar and a little vanilla and ice cream was in the making.

Tub baths were a weekly affair, usually on Saturday, but Mama insisted on each of us taking what she called a "spit bath" nightly. Spit baths were taken in the gallon or so of water which filled the gray enamel wash pan, aided by a wash rag and a bar of Life Buoy soap. The icy water of Yocum Creek occasionally provided a welcome alternative.

Now, after a daily shower, I scramble from my air-conditioned house into an air-conditioned car and head for town. How did we survive the summers of yesterday?

For most of us who grew up in this area amidst the innocence of playmates and unspoiled natural beauty of our hills, with loving parents, we knew we could always depend on, I think most of us would answer, "Very well, thank you!"

70

Hay Season Makes
For Stressful Living

Look at the birds of the air; they do not sow or reap or store away
in barns, and yet your heavenly Father feeds them. Are you not
more valuable than they? Matthew 6:26

Whoever said that country living is stress-free never lived where I live. This is haying season in the Arkansas Ozarks.

It looks pastoral and peaceful. Cattle appear to float across a field of swaying fescue. The songs of meadowlarks and chuck-will-widows echo across the sweet smelling countryside.

But in the little pumpkin-yellow pickup truck bouncing about our farm, one does not find a placid spirit. Far from it.

"If the hay men don't get here today we will lose the hop clover for sure," my husband remarks glumly, as he leans out of the window of the slow moving vehicle to study the ground.

I grew up on a farm. Among my first memories is my Daddy making similar dire predictions about the highly desirable, but incredibly fragile hop clover.

If the mowers arrive on schedule there is still curing, baling, hauling, and stacking hay to be gotten through.

I have a permanent crick in my neck from the time my husband was looking at the threatening clouds hovering over a field of freshly mown hay. We crossed a pond ditch just east of the house at somewhat less than a safe speed. The words I uttered after my head bounced against the top of the pickup truck a couple of times will not be repeated here.

If one opts for the old-fashioned small, oblong bales instead of the popular round ones (no haulers required) we have another stress maker. They are called hay haulers. They are hard to find, they are expensive, and some don't know beans about stacking hay. We have been fortunate in recent years as my husband's nephews, who are the best haulers around, have helped us out.

Take my advice. Don't come to the country in May for some R & R. Instead, try a goat roping or a rooster fight.

First Rate Dad

A wise son heeds his father's instructions. Proverbs 13:1

Life is a matter of choices. I have made some good ones. I have made some bad ones. But the best one I ever made, was in choosing a father for my children.

A man of few words my husband taught the children by example. He was a hard worker as he expected them to be. Many of the skills he taught them twenty-five or thirty years ago are now nearly obsolete.

He taught the boys how to set a cedar fence post, how to dehorn and castrate cattle, and how to stack hay so it wouldn't fall. Skills not too much in demand in the sixties and even less in demand today, but knowing how to do a job right and to not give up never goes out of style.

The children's father had had rowdy days before we were married, but never again. "I never want to be responsible for doing something in front of the children that I wouldn't want them to do," he explained.

The kids biggest cheerleader was their Dad. We drove hundreds of miles and sat through countless sporting events during the years our children were at home. My husband held down a full-time job, milked cows twice a day and still found time to coach the Little League team on which our boys played.

With few words their father managed to get across to the children the value of an education. No one got paid for good grades. One was expected to do their best, and that was reward enough.

Don't get me wrong. We were not the Waltons, or Little House on the Prairie. We have had our share of problems, but having a father to look up to has helped.

My husband's Great-Grandmother was a full-blooded Cherokee, a heritage which gives both my husband and children thick dark hair and high cheekbones. The kids like this.

In fact, my daughter's card to her father on his recent birthday read, "With you around, it's no wonder the rest of us are just Indians: Happy Birthday to the Chief." I am glad I chose well.

Ella Marie

Blessed are the dead who die in the Lord. Revelation 14:13

The back seat of Daddy's thirty-six Ford held a hoe, a rake, eighteen assorted glass jars filled with flowers, a gallon jug of well water, the sweet, cloying odor of peonies, and a nine-year-old girl. That was me. It was Decoration Day in the mountains of northwest Arkansas and we were headed for the cemetery. I bounced on the lumpy seat in joyful anticipation.

"Well, where do you want to start, Mae?" Daddy asked Mama as he carefully eased the car out of the yard and started down the steep hill to State Road 103, a bumpy path to the Pickens Cemetery.

Of course, Daddy knew what Mama's answer would be. We always went to Pickens Cemetery first. That was where the babies were buried, boys, one whose tiny headstone bore the inscription "Baby Boy Stafford born November 20, 1919, died November 20, 1919." The other grave belonged to Billy Ray, who died of whooping cough at one month despite Dr. Donaldson's best efforts to save him.

Going to the cemeteries, Pickens and Glenwood, where an assortment of aunts, uncles, cousins and grandparents lay buried was one of spring's special delights to me. I loved hearing the stories, repeated in a yearly ritual, of how they lived and how they died.

Helping Daddy clean off each grave and then carefully carrying Mama's bouquets of roses, iris, peonies, snowballs and always the wild daisies to adorn each grave, was not only fun, but satisfying.

The saddest grave was Ella Marie's in Marionville, MO. We didn't go there every year, but I think Grandpa did.

Ella Marie, a beautiful, well-educated girl (for that time) married my Grandfather when she was seventeen and he was twenty. Two years later my Daddy was born. It was then that Ella Marie became a victim of one of the mysterious maladies of that day, sometimes called "childbirth fever". She died nine months later.

Her dying request was that she be buried in the old part of the cemetery. "It would be too lonely in the new part," she said.

My Grandfather remarried twice more. He fathered other children and became a prosperous business man. He was an organizer of the present First National Bank of Green Forest. He was also Carroll County Judge as well as State Representative from our district.

But in the springtime, when the flowers were speaking most eloquently and Memorial Day was near, Grandpa drove, sometimes alone, sometimes with a grandchild or two, to Marionville. There he placed flowers on th' grave of Ella Marie.

Grandkids

Creating Memories
Spring '91

Children's children are a crown to the aged. Proverbs 17:6A

Five years ago this month our first grandson was born. We came to grandparenting late in life and immediately made complete fools of ourselves. Fortunately, the Lord saw fit for John-Mark to have a brother born nineteen months later. Dylan diffused the attention we were lavishing on his brother.

The boys live with their parents in a city nearly two hundred miles away, but John-Mark's heart is attached to Nubbin Ridge. He thinks my husband, his beloved "Pa", at five-foot-ten, is the largest person he has ever seen.

Pa and John-Mark have never talked "little kid" talk. They speak of cows freshening, hay needing to be hauled, bull buying and stock trailer repairs.

Although our grandson will wear Nikes and shirts with alligators on them to his preschool, he wouldn't be caught dead in such a getup when he is on Nubbin Ridge.

Apparel worn here is as much like Pa's as possible; blue jeans, cowboy boots, and always, winter and summer, a straw Stetson. Even his voice deepens, in an unconscious effort to talk more like Pa.

As the years go by John-Mark will probably learn from Pa how to dehorn and castrate a calf, how to build a fence, and how to tell when a cow is near calving.

What good will the skills learned on Nubbin Ridge be to a young man whose entire adult life will be lived in the 21st century? Some might say, "very little."

The skills may be forgotten, but the grandfather who loved a five-year old boy enough to treat him as an adult, will never be.

Making A Trade
1992

*My son, if thine heart be wise, my heart shall rejoice,
even mine. Proverbs 23:15*

When six-year-old John-Mark arrived last weekend with his parents and little brother, his cow, a large Santa Gertrudis, had just given birth. Our grandson was ecstatic. He hastened to inform me that it was not a calf, it was a bull, which his cow had had.

His enthusiasm rivalled that of his grandfather's two weeks earlier when a rather non-descript little black baldy cow not only had twin calves but immediately bonded with each of them and seemed to have plenty of milk to raise them.

The birth of John-Mark's calf was difficult. The calf was large and beautiful but even with an assisted birth he had breathing problems, and difficulty standing.

"I really like my calf," John-Mark confided the next day, after yet another trip to the barn. "He lets me pet him." The cow, who was, as my husband said, "a little waspy," had to be put in the headgate when the calf was held up to her to allow it to nurse. She was fiercely devoted to her baby but not to the humans who were assisting him.

By Saturday night the new born was unable to stand. He was given milk from a bottle. My daughter and her husband worked tirelessly in an attempt to save him.

On Sunday we all realized that the calf was not going to make it. All of us but John-Mark that is. He was still petting the calf, talking to it, and believing that it would soon be alright.

Pa finally got him, John-Mark, in the pickup and drove him down in the pasture to see the black baldy and her twins. "Son," Pa said, "How would you like to trade your calf for my set of twins?" If anyone was a loser Pa wanted it to be himself, not this grandson with whom he had always had an almost mystical bond.

"No, Pa, not now," John-Mark explained patiently. "But if my calf dies I will sure trade with you."

Here Come the Inspectors!
1993

The father of the righteous shall greatly rejoice; and he that begetteth a wise child shall have joy of him. Proverbs 23:24

The inspectors were here last weekend. We hadn't seen them for a couple of months. They climbed out of the van and hit the road running toward our front door. They are our grandsons, Dylan, age six and John-Mark, seven.

The inspectors ask many questions. "Why did you unplug our Nintendo?" they want to know. "Because neither Pa nor I could figure out how to play it," I explained.

They examine a first book of geography and a plastic globe I have for them. "Why did you get this thing, Ne-Ne?" they asked. "Because I didn't want you to grow up to be geographical illiterates like I am. I never went anywhere, I never saw anything, when I was little like you. Lovett's Pond, north of the Cisco community was the largest body of water I had ever seen," I replied.

They make short work of placing the forty or so stickers on the globe. Neither Pa nor I are much help. "How come you and Pa don't know where the Suez Canal is?" the inspectors ask.

On Saturday we introduce Bo, the new colt to the boys. "Nice horse," Dylan comments. "Is it a boy or a girl or what?" he asks. "Son," Pa replies, "This little horse is a stallion."

Dylan turns to me, "What's a stallion, Ne-Ne?" Before I can assemble my scattering thoughts Dylan answers his own question. "I know, I know! A stallion is the horse that can run the fastest."

John-Mark who has had trouble with reading but seemed to arrive on this earth able to count says, "Pa, what did you have to pay for the little horse?" Pa tells him. John-Mark gazes reflectively on the horses for a few minutes before he asks, "Did you pay cash or use a credit card?"

And A Child Shall Lead Them
Spring '94

Lo, children are a heritage of the Lord. Psalm 127:3

"One of the most obvious facts about grown-ups to a child is that they have forgotten how to be a child," someone once said. Our grandson, Dylan, age six, helps us to recall those childhood days.

Dylan not only enjoys being a kid, he likes to share his joy with others. "Hi, Ne-Ne!" he calls as I enter the bathroom where he sits, chest-deep, in soap suds. "Can you stay for tea?"

Carefully arranged around the rim of the tub Dylan has placed four tiny plastic cups resting on matching saucers, and a pink flowered teapot.

Settling myself on the only stool available, green porcelain to match the tub, Dylan and I have a tea party.

Later my grandson introduces me to a new game. It cannot be bought at Wal-Mart or Toys R Us. Dylan made up the rules and owns the only playing pieces. He calls the game cow-bowling.

Tiny cows, brought by Santa Claus to our grown-up son when he was young, are arranged like bowling pins. Dylan announces that we will use a piece of round wood about the size of a water glass as our ball.

I am handed the wobbly wood and told to hit a strike. I can't. He can and we both laugh.

Dylan is a digger. City lawns are different from country yards. At home in Kansas City he does not dig. On Nubbin Ridge he does. Tools vary, sometimes a sharp stick, other times Pa's shovel.

The size of the hole is of little consequence to Dylan. It is what he might uncover that brings a sparkle to his brown eyes.

"Look Ne-Ne," he calls to me in my shady spot under the box elder, "A worm!" In the parched soil of late autumn, he pulls forth an earthworm, which he places carefully in a margarine tub to carry home to Kansas.

The old hill is quiet now. The little boys are gone. But sometimes when I round a corner of the house in a hurried pursuit of "busyness" it seems I catch a glimpse of that little boy and hear once again his voice, "Come Ne-Ne, look!" For a moment I stop and become a child again.

Dylan's Miracle
Spring '95

You are the God who performs miracles; you display your
power among the peoples. Psalm 77:13

Webster defines miracle as, "an act of God, a remarkable event or thing." Grandson Dylan, age seven, and I have both laid claim to miracles in recent weeks.

Dylan's miracle happened the day he played sick and convinced his mother he wasn't able to attend school.

After an hour or so alone in his room (his mother, whom he may not have convinced after all, insisted that sick children must stay in bed) Dylan was bored and lonely. His big brother along with the four children next door were in school. The neighborhood was quiet.

"Guess what? I feel better now," Dylan called downstairs to his mother. After feeding the recent invalid a peanut butter and jelly sandwich and a glass of milk, his mother drove him to school.

As the smiling little boy alighted from the car he turned back to give his mother a kiss and said, "You know what, Mom, I was really sick just this morning and now I am well. It was a miracle!"

My miracle was longer in coming than Dylan's. It started five years ago when I suffered a retinal detachment. Vision that was always poor became a little more so. Gradually over the years a cataract developed and I became legally blind in my left eye.

I was told that the cataract could never be removed due to the possibility of another retinal detachment. However, with everything to gain and nothing to lose and with the encouragement of a new opthomologist I underwent cataract surgery yesterday morning as an outpatient at the local hospital and received a lens implant.

This morning the bandage was removed and sight had been restored. Just like Dylan I can only say, "It was a miracle!" A miracle because many were praying and most of all a miracle from the One who, with a touch, restored sight long ago and still does today.

Keeping Fit With Your Grandchildren
Summer '96

*Fathers, provoke not your children to anger, lest they
be discouraged. Colossians 3:21*

The grandsons are coming. Schools out you know. They are nice little boys who live in a large city. We live not exactly at the end of the world but one can see it from our deck. The boys are ages eight and ten. We are much older. Our life-styles are as different as Billy Graham and Dennis Rodman.

One major difference is the energy thing. They have it. Their Grandfather and I do not. Their idea of a fun day is a couple of trips to the nearest Wal-Mart (eighteen miles round trip from our house) riding Topsy, the pony, swimming in Yocum Creek, playing chase, cars, dominoes, Nintendo and wrestling.

A good day for Pa and myself is a trip to the mailbox, watching Tom Dye's weather report on TV, taking a couple of recliner naps and eventually going to bed.

Obviously the only way to cope with this active pair is to get into shape, much like preparing for the Olympics.

The first step in the fitness regimen will be pushing ourselves out of our recliners. But then what? How does one become physically fit on a cattle farm when one's sagging body is lower than the price of yearlings?

Pa thinks we might cut thistles, he with a bushhog and I with a hoe. I'd need a trainer to prepare for that.

"Why not just practice doing what the boys usually do on a typical day," I suggest. "That must be what makes them so peppy."

So tomorrow we start training. When we wake up we will sit in bed in our underwear playing NBA Jam on the Nintendo for a couple of hours, followed by running through the house jumping high in an attempt to reach a ceiling fan pull cord. In the afternoon we will get a couple of shovels and dig holes in the backyard, holes which we will eventually fill with water.

If you read in the newspaper next week that our friends are walking slow and singing low as they pass our prostrate bodies you will know the fitness plan failed. On well, everybody has to go sometime!

Staying Alive, Staying Alive . . .
Spring '97

Correct thy son, and he shall give thee rest; yea, he shall delight thy soul. Proverbs 29:17

Our grandsons are as different as John Wayne and Woody Allen. John-Mark, who just turned eleven, is an outdoorsman, blonde, polite, handsome, popular, with an eye for the girls.

Dylan, age nine, can do without cowboying, camping or girls. His hair is dark, big brown eyes peer from behind spectacles; he is fascinated with words, and uses one at every opportunity.

Dylan came into the house last week to report on his older brother's most recent misdoing. "John-Mark is talking dirty," he said.

"What did he say?" his mother asked.

"He said the D word," Dylan replied. "You know, the word that means to hold the water back, but it was the other D word he said."

And then, before his mother could step outside to counsel his brother, Dylan explained, "Actually, I said the D word, too, but I meant the kind that holds back water."

When the boys and their mother spent spring break on our hill, Dylan opted to go shopping with the women folk rather than help his brother, Pa, and uncle work cattle. After some mall shopping, the three of us stopped by McGuffey's for lunch.

I was delighted to find a box of crayons and a drawing on our table, just waiting to be colored. "Look Dylan!" I exclaimed. "You can color while we wait for our food."

Instead, that kid talked and he talked, not about normal stuff, but about mammals in Australia, which oceans border which continent, and heaven knows what else. Finally, when he picked up a table knife and said, "Ne-Ne, did you know this knife is a wedge which has been inserted into an inclined plane?", I grabbed that box of crayons and went to work. Somebody had to be a kid, and it wasn't Dylan.

Next day when the Tribune arrived I pointed out my column, Nubbin Ridge, to my youngest grandson. He was obviously unimpressed, as he said, "Actually, Ne-Ne, I don't like this story very well, but the good thing is it gives you something to do, and old people who keep busy live longer, you know."

Mama's
Scrapbook

A Tribute to Grandmother

By Mama's oldest Grandchild
Sue Oxford Towns.

We now live in the age of "airport grandmothers". At Christmas time we pick them up at the airport. When their visit ends we deposit them back at the airport. Grandmothers don't always know the names of the latest toys, so rather than be wrong they send a check to more than cover the cost of whatever is in fashion at the time.

But let me tell you of a time when Grandmother had never been on an airplane, and many had never even been to the airport. It was a time that the poet Mildred R. Grenier describes in . . .

WALKING WITH GRANDMA

"I like to walk with Grandma,
Her steps are short like mine.
She doesn't say 'Now hurry up',
She always takes her time."

"I like to walk with Grandma,
Her eyes see things mine do –
Wee pebbles bright, a funny cloud,
Half hidden drops of dew."

"Most people have to hurry;
They do not stop and see
I'm glad that God made Grandmas
Unrushed and young like me."

It was in the late 1930's that we drove to Grandmother's house in the heat of summer and in an auto with no air conditioner. But it was not the heat that made the trip seem long, it was the anxious little minds and hearts wondering what Grandmother would be doing. She was the most interesting person that we knew.

Bounding out of the car and into the house meant one thing most of all – – surprises to delight the heart of any child. No, there were no new toys or games, at least not the kind that can be bought in a store. However, there might be the smell of chocolate fudge still bubbling on the stove. Of course, it had somehow just cooked to testing stage as we walked into the house. Grandmother let us be the judge. Was it time to pour the thick hot chocolate onto the buttered platter? Should it cook just a little longer? She trusted us! And what if our appetite for that sweet goodness got the better of our good judgement. Well, we ate it with a spoon! Without her ever having said a word, we had learned something about patience, cooking, chemistry, and temperature, all in one lesson.

And as we licked the spoons of their last morsel of sweetness, Grandmother began to recite the poems that she knew we loved to hear. Some were funny, and she laughed as hard as we did. Some were sad, and some of us cried. Many more than I realized then, taught us the lessons that we would need in life. Surely no other unschooled farm woman in the 1930's could have loved literature more, nor could have memorized more poetry than she. But it was in sharing her gift that made our lives rich. And now that memory makes this chapter of this book possible.

The following poems are a few of the many that she loved. These are the ones that she clipped from the DROVERS TELEGRAM and others from the KANSAS CITY STAR, along with those she learned from the McGUFFEY'S READER.

Mother's Hands

To look upon my mother's hands
And her life there see . . .
Aging hours . . . lines of love
Spent in molding me.

I know these hands, the work they've done,
Now grown old from toil.
I know the beauty in flowers they grew
And how they loved God's soil.

I remember the times they've comforted me;
Helped me along the way
And clasped together, humble with faith,
In prayer at the end of each day.

These hands, no longer mine to hold,
Their duties do not shirk
For they are young and busy still,
In Heaven . . . with God's work.

Marilyn Louderback

Which Loved Best?

"I love you, Mother," said little John;
Then, forgetting work, his cap went on,
And he was off to the garden swing,
Leaving his mother the wood to bring.

"I love you, Mother," said rosy Nell;
"I love you better than tongue can tell;"
Then she teased and pouted full half the day,
Till her mother rejoiced when she went to play.

"I love you, Mother," said little Fan;
"Today I'll help you all I can;
How glad I am that school doesn't keep!"
So she rocked the baby till it fell asleep.

Then, stepping softly, she took the broom,
And swept the floor, and dusted the room;
Busy and happy all day was she,
Helpful and cheerful as child could be.

"I love you, mother," again they said –
Three little children going to bed;
How do you think that mother guessed
Which of them really loved her best?

Joy Allison
McGuffey's Third Reader

Forty Years Ago

I've wandered to the village, Tom,
 I've sat beneath the tree,
Upon the schoolhouse playground,
 That sheltered you and me;
But none were left to greet me, Tom,
 And few were left to know,
Who played with me upon the green,
 Just forty years ago.

The grass was just as green, Tom,
 Barefooted boys at play
Were sporting, just as we did then,
 With spirits just as gay.
But the master sleeps upon the hill,
 Which, coated o'er with snow,
Afforded us a sliding place,
 Some forty years ago.

The old schoolhouse is altered some;
 The benches are replaced
By new ones very like the same
 Our jackknives had defaced.
But the same old bricks are in the wall,
 The bell swings to and fro;
It music's just the same, dear Tom,
 'Twas forty years ago.

– Author unknown
McGuffey's Fifth Reader

Promises

God hath not promised
Skies always blue,
Flower-strewn pathways
All our lives thru;
God hath not promised
Sun without rain,
Joy without sorrow,
Peace without pain.

But, God hath promised
Strength for the day,
Rest for the labor,
Light for the way,
Grace for the trials,
Help from above,
Unfailing sympathy,
Undying love.

– Author unknown

Old Friends

New Friends I cherish, and treasure their worth,
But old friends to me are the salt of the earth.
Friends are like garments that everyone wears –
New ones are needed for dress-up affairs,
But when we're at leisure, we're more apt to choose
The clothes that we purchased with last season's shoes.
Things we grow used to are things we love best –
The ones we are certain have weathered the best.
And isn't it true, since we're talking of friends,
That new ones bring pleasure when everything blends,
But when we want someone who thinks as we do
And who fits, as I said, like last summer's shoe,
We turn to the friends who have stuck thru' the years,
Who echo our laughter and dry our tears;
They know every weakness and fault we possess,
But somehow forget them in friendship's caress,
The story is old, yet fragrant and sweet,
I've said it before, but just let me repeat;
New friends I cherish, and treasure their worth
But old friends to me are the salt of the earth.

– Author unknown

Blue Print

I love an old house
With trees in its hair
And grass that needs cutting
And doesn't much care,
Kittens and crickets
And sunshine and snow,
Old mended places
That don't hardly show –
I love an old house
With dusk in its eye
That can't keep from dreaming
And doesn't much try.

– Gladys Martin

Hearts of Love

I'm wrapping up this valentine,
And sending it to you,
Your Mommy made it years ago,
With love so sweet and true,
The printed word of love's still there,
Although a wee bit dim.
The red heart too has faded some,
Placed there in childish whim.
Your Mommy, once a little girl,
Was mine, like you're her boy.
Her tears and hurts I kissed away.
Like she cures yours with joy.
Our love together through the years,
Has brought me endless joy.
Now I've another heart to love,
My Grandson! Mommy's boy.

– Isabel Wilson

Beatitudes of an Aged One

Blessed are they who understand
My faltering steps and paising hand.
Blessed are they who know my ears today
Must strain to catch the things they say.

Blessed are they who seem to know
My eyes are dim and my wits are slow.
Blessed are they with a cheery smile
Who stop to chat for a little while.

Blessed are they who know the ways
To bring back memories of yesterdays.
Blessed are they who know I'm at a loss
to find the strength to carry the Cross.

Blessed are they who ease the days
On my journey Home in loving ways.

– Author unknown

If I Had Known

If I had known in the morning
How wearily all the day
The words unkind
Would trouble my mind
I said when you went away,
I had been more careful, darling,
Nor given you needless pain,
But we vex our own
With look and tone,
We might never take back again.

For though in the quiet evening
You may give me the kiss of peace,
Yet it might be
That never for me
The pain of the heart should cease.
How many go forth in the morning
Who never come home at night?
And hearts have broken
For harsh words spoken,
That sorrow can never set right.

We have careful thoughts for the stranger,
And smiles for the sometimes guest,
But oft for our own
The bitter tone,
Though we love our own the best.
Ah! lips with the curve impatient,
Oh! brow with that look of scorn;
'Twer a cruel fate
Were the night too late
To undo the work of the morn.

– Author unknown

The Friend Who Stands By

When troubles come your soul to try,
You love the friend who just stands by.
Perhaps there's nothing he can do;
The things are strictly up to you,
For there are troubles all your own,
And paths the soul must tread alone;
Times when love can't smooth the road,
Nor friendship lift the heavy load.

But just to feel you have a friend,
Who will stand by until the end;
Whose sympathy through all endures,
Whose warm handclasp is always yours.
It helps somewhat to pull you through,
although there's nothing he can do;
And so with fervent heart we cry,
"God bless the friend who just stands by."

– Author unknown

Featherstitched Poem

Dear Great-Aunt Miranda
Made a poem they say,
Light as schoolgirl fancy,
Bright and warm and gay.

Dear Great-Aunt Miranda
Could not read or write,
Yet her poem, feather-stitched,
Warms me every night.

Every phrase from silver pen,
Lilting heart-beat thrill
Captured in her patchwork quilt
With her needle-quill.

– Maggie Culver Fry

She Walks by Night

My mother walked by night, and where she passed,
contentment spread, and safety, for her hand brought magic
to a pillow. She would stand before a window, making
shutters fast against a midnight storm, her love a shield no
javelin of light could force to yield. Safe in her presence,
certain she would keep all evil out, I gave myself to sleep.

Now as I walk from room to room at night, smoothing
the covers of a restless child, or closing shutters when the
night is wild, to keep at bay the storm's unearthly light,
a quiet step accompanies my own, and in the dark I do not
walk alone.

– Goldie Capers Smith

Just for Today

In the midst of the trials and troubles
That seem to beset my way,
Help me to remember to thank You, Lord,
For the privilege of living today.

Keep me from dwelling on those things
I feel life has denied to me
Cause me to see that all is well
If each day I walk with Thee.

Perhaps what I wanted most, dear Lord,
Was not Your will for me,
So even though my dreams are gone,
Yet my faith remains in Thee.

It's not my failures that matter most
Nor how often I fall on the way,
What really counts is what I do
With the time given me today.

So, keep me faithful in what'er task
You may find for me to do,
Whether it be small or large,
May I do it well for You.

– Author unknown

The Old Work Harness

They tore the old barn down today
To make a tractor shed;
The barn we built so long ago,
The year that we were wed.

I went down there to say "Good-bye,"
The old barn was my friend,
And it is due to pay respect
At any journey's end.

I know that change must come to all,
Must come to everything,
And foolish 'tis in summer's time
To try to hold the spring.

The stalls were still quite strong and true,
The feed boxes still held
Some scattering cobs, which the strong teeth
Of Dick and Barney shelled.

In a dark corner on its side
There lay a stout nail keg.
And in its nested prairie hay
I saw a china egg.

On the back wall, on wooden pegs
The work team's harness hung –
Saddest of all these souvenirs
Of years when I was young.

The poor, lost thing who hung them there,
Wakes never from his sleeping,
And I, who am a quiet one,
Was torn with sudden weeping.

– Author unknown

Too Old to Cry

(A mother's thoughts on seeing her son go through agonies of losing his dog.)

She loved the lad, He loved her, too.
He was fourteen, she, only two.
Where'er she went, he need but call
She followed close behind.

When troubles came to him
She sympathized, no questions asked.
She blindly followed where he led.

When school bells rang
She mutely watched him go,
Her world collapsed! Her friend was gone!

When he came home, she cried.
Her master knelt and hugged her close
And she was reassured.

One day she went to meet the bus,
No other thought in mind.
A car came quickly from the west
And she was dead.

Her master's grief was deep,
He must not weep.
"Too old to cry," but curly head bent low
To hide the tears that trickled down.

He gently lifted her and held her in his arms
Till she was cold.
His face was streaked with tears and eyes were red.

He laid his dog to rest beneath the trees
Where summer sun could never pry,
Nor winter winds their chilling fingers clutch.

He never talks about the fun the two had had.
But when he looks toward her grave
We know his thoughts are with her there,
He does not speak – he daren't,
He's too old to cry.

– Author unknown

The Wheel Turns

Where did my "ducklings" go so fast –?
Toddlers, teen-agers, grown up at last,
I walk along through the garden late,
I see a kite string wound round the gate;
A bicycle handle, a wagon wheel bent;
Memories still linger, my cowboys – went.

A tear falls now – my steps grow slow,
Where, oh, where did my plaid shirts go?
I go back to the house – it's only a house,
No fun, no laughter, it's still as a mouse.
The phone sets ghost-like, radio too;
I walk to the door, nothing to do.

My husband is home, he greets with a bow,
I said "You're all that's left for me now."
He smiled, I might know he'd say something smart,
"You know I was all you had at the start."

– Jewell McDaniel

A Journey

Life is like a journey on a train,
With two fellow-travelers at each window pane.
I may sit beside you all the journey through,
Or I may sit elsewhere, never knowing you.
But should fate make me to sit by your side,
Let's be pleasant travelers, 'tis so short a ride.

– Author unknown

The Better Way

I'd rather see a sermon
than hear one any day;
I'd rather one should walk with me,
than merely show the way.

The eye's a better pupil
and more willing than the ear;
Fine counsel is confusing,
but example's always clear.

And the best of all the preachers
are the men who live their creeds,
For to see the good in action
is what everybody needs.

I can soon learn how to do it
if you'll let me see it done.
I can watch your hands in action
but your tongue too fast may run.

And the lectures you deliver
may be very wise and true,
But I'd rather get my lesson
by observing what you do.

For I may misunderstand you,
and the high advice you give,
But there's no misunderstanding
how you act and how you live.

– Author unknown

Talk Happiness

Talk happiness!
Not now and then, but every Blessed day,
Even if you don't believe
The half of what You say;
There's no room here for him
Who whines as on his way he goes;
Remember, son, the world is
Sad enough without your woes.

Talk happiness each chance You get – and
Talk it good and strong;
Look for it in the byways
as you grimly plod along;
Perhaps it is a stranger now
Whose visit never comes;
But talk it! Soon you'll find
That you and Happiness
Are chums.

– Author unknown

101

About The Author

Fayrene Stafford Farmer was born, reared and continues to live in Carroll County, Arkansas, deep in the heart of her beloved Ozark Mountains.

A graduate of the University of Arkansas, she is a retired schoolteacher and a full-time farm wife. She has had articles published in various newspapers and magazines including FARM JOURNAL, PARENTS MAGAZINE, JOURNAL OF BUSINESS EDUCATION, SPRINGFIELD DAILY NEWS, ARKANSAS GAZETTE, ARKANSAS DEMOCRAT AND OZARK MOUNTAINEER.

She has written a popular column for Carroll County Newspapers for several years entitled Nubbin Ridge.

To send for additional copies of

The Home Place

cut and fill out form at bottom.
Send check or money order to:

Fayrene Stafford Farmer
5423 CR 601
Green Forest, AR 72638

ORDER FORM - THE HOME PLACE

Name: _____

Address: _____

City: _____ State _____ Zip _____

Phone: (_____) _____

Please send me _____ copy(s) of "The Home Place"

    Cost (Per book) .... $7.95 _____

    Shipping & Handling (ea.)....... $2.00 _____

                                       Total _____